SPECIAL DUTIES PILOT

THE MAN WHO FLEW THE *REAL* 'INGLOURIOUS BASTERDS'
BEHIND ENEMY LINES

To Barbara and Fred

SPECIAL DUTIES PILOT

THE MAN WHO FLEW THE *REAL* 'INGLOURIOUS BASTERDS' BEHIND ENEMY LINES

JOHN M. BILLINGS

AIR WORLD

AIR WORLD

SPECIAL DUTIES PILOT
THE MAN WHO FLEW THE *REAL* 'INGLOURIOUS BASTERDS'
BEHIND ENEMY LINES

First published in Great Britain in 2021 by
Air World
An imprint of
Pen & Sword Books Ltd
Yorkshire – Philadelphia

ISBN 978 1 52678 626 5

A CIP catalogue record for this book is available from the British Library.

Typeset by SJmagic DESIGN SERVICES, India.

Printed and bound in the UK by TJ Books Ltd.

Pen & Sword Books Limited incorporates the imprints of Atlas, Archaeology, Aviation, Discovery, Family History, Fiction, History, Maritime, Military, Military Classics, Politics, Select, Transport, True Crime, Air World, Frontline Publishing, Leo Cooper, Remember When, Seaforth Publishing, The Praetorian Press, Wharncliffe Local History, Wharncliffe Transport, Wharncliffe True Crime and White Owl.

For a complete list of Pen & Sword titles please contact

PEN & SWORD BOOKS LIMITED
47 Church Street, Barnsley, South Yorkshire, S70 2AS, England
E-mail: enquiries@pen-and-sword.co.uk
Website: www.pen-and-sword.co.uk

Or
PEN AND SWORD BOOKS
1950 Lawrence Rd, Havertown, PA 19083, USA
E-mail: Uspen-and-sword@casematepublishers.com
Website: www.penandswordbooks.com

MIX
Paper from
responsible sources
FSC® C013056
www.fsc.org

Contents

Foreword

This unforgettable and historically significant autobiography includes a quote from a 1945 film made by the U.S. Army Air Forces, *Wings for This Man*: "A fighter pilot is a combination of a mathematician and an athlete, a scientist and a sharpshooter. He's got to know what goes on inside his plane. The heart of his fighter is steel and copper; its bloodstream is gas and oil. But its brain is the man who flies it." Captain John Billings is all these things and something more: a gifted storyteller.

Billings is an incredibly skilled and fearless pilot who flew fifty-three missions during World War II. They included thirty-nine missions for the Office of Strategic Services (OSS), the predecessor to the CIA and the U.S. Special Operations Command, flying alone and at altitudes as low as 300 feet to deliver agents and supplies behind enemy lines. In one of the war's most daring operations, he dropped Fred Mayer – the real "inglourious basterd" – onto a lake 10,000 feet above sea level in the Austrian Alps. He tells these harrowing stories with a calmness and humility that are common characteristics among OSS veterans who performed acts of unparalleled bravery. John Billings beat the odds and survived the war. For many years, he has been flying "Angel Flights" that provide free air travel to patients in need of specialized medical care. Having beat the odds himself, he has dedicated his life to helping others beat the odds, too.

This book's title, *Special Duties Pilot*, could just as easily have been *Born to Fly*, which he recognized was his destiny from a very young age. How very fortunate for the United States that he was able to fulfill it.

Charles Pinck, President
The OSS Society

Acknowledgments

There are two people whose dedication should be noted for this book. Without them it would not have happened.

Suzanne Rhodes listened to my memories over the phone for hours and spent a full weekend at our home in Virginia, listening and writing furiously as I talked. She asked important questions and then allowed me to run with the memories those questions raised to the surface. She was so careful to get things right. Somehow, she made sense of all the disconnected pieces of memories that came pouring out from so long ago. Then she put the puzzle together in readable form. The best way to describe her is amazing. Thank you, Suzanne.

The other person to note is Charles Pinck, President of the OSS Society. He was the one who contacted and negotiated with publishers. I have absolutely no idea how all of this was done. However, in good OSS fashion, he completed the mission in getting this book published and never shared a clue as to how it was done. Thank you, Charles.

John M. Billings

Introduction

As a friend and fellow pilot, I'm pleased to write the introduction to *Special Duties Pilot,* the true story of the amazing John Billings. When I think of John, the word "wingspan" comes to mind for the many decades he has spent in the sky, and also for the span of his tremendous character qualities and achievements, which I am honored to name and describe.

Passion
Since his first airplane ride in 1926 at the age of three, John has exhibited a rarely-equaled excitement and love for flying – and for life. This passion is unstoppable, even at age ninety-seven. Whether commanding a B-24 Liberator bomber, a DC-3, a DC-9, or a Cessna Cutlass 172RG, John was born to fly.

Leader
Soon after John's enlistment in the U.S. Army Air Forces in 1942 at age eighteen, those in charge recognized him as not only an excellent pilot but also as a gifted leader. At age twenty, he was assigned as command pilot for the B-24 Liberator bomber with a crew of nine. His leadership skills continued throughout the war and through his extensive airline career.

Hero
From 1944 to 1945, John led his aircraft and crew safely through fifty-three combat missions over Europe. Most of these were night-time, covert flights inserting spies behind Nazi lines. This is a classic example of heroism from our "Greatest Generation."

Captain
Upon leaving his distinguished military service, John went on to fly for TWA and then for Eastern Airlines. He captained many types of commercial aircraft before retiring in 1983.

SPECIAL DUTIES PILOT

Volunteer

In addition to offering his flying and leadership skills for dangerous covert missions during World War II, John has been a volunteer pilot with Angel Flight Mid-Atlantic since 2005. While using his own aircraft and paying all expenses, he has provided free transportation for patients and veterans to distant medical evaluation and treatment. As of March 2020, he has completed more than 450 Angel Flights.

Mentor

John has provided guidance and encouragement to dozens of aspiring pilots over his long career.

Joyful

John is a man full of joy who is thankful for his long and productive life. I have never seen him without his huge, warm smile.

*****

Special Duties Pilot is told with humor, intelligence, and kindness. It's a treasure of a book that will keep you engrossed from beginning to end.

Steve Craven

Author's Note

The stories in this book are true stories. Either I participated in them, witnessed them, or heard them from others – and in the latter case, they were verified by more than one source.

Chapter 1

Love at First Flight

At an early age, I realized my memory was more remarkable than most. Once I asked my mother about the blue flame stove. "What you remember," she said, "is a kitchen stove. It was kerosene fired and used canisters inside that made the blue flame shine through isinglass. And you weren't even six months old! That was the only time we had a stove like that."

The blue flame. It's the fire for flight my father kindled in my heart from a very young age, an impulse that tugs at me when my feet have been on the ground too long and I've got to be sky-borne. Alson Powers Billings loved airplanes. On my third birthday, August 7, 1926, he bought two tickets at three dollars each for an airplane ride at the local airfield in Hingham, Massachusetts. I really do mean it was a field – a square patch about a third of a mile on a side where grass struggled to grow and a sign that read, "Air Rides Here."

The plane was a Curtiss Robin Cabin Class, with a big radial engine in front. A man hopped up on the left wheel, pushed a crank into the engine's side, and turned it briskly. Like magic in the eyes of a small boy, the engine came alive with a small puff of smoke and a loud roar. A crowd was standing by, eagerly watching the co-pilot as he climbed into the right seat and planted me in his lap. Dad was friends with the pilot, and no one back then had to worry about the FAA. If you made the same number of landings as you made take-offs, you satisfied all the rules. I remember the amazement I felt seeing the tiny houses and toy trains far below. The trip probably lasted no more than ten or fifteen minutes, but it seemed like an entire day to me because I was taking in so much land and sky. All too soon it was over, but it's still with me, that vivid memory of when my lust to fly was awakened.

The six dollars spent on those tickets by my father were hard-earned and precious. He was a millwright and worked for the Welch Company Lumber Mill in Scituate, Massachusetts, our seaside town in Plymouth County.

As the only employee, he ran the mill and worked forty-eight hours a week. He could do anything and everything, including grinding knives to a pattern to satisfy a contractor's wish for molding of one shape or another. Every Saturday evening, he would come home with his pay envelope and empty it on the kitchen table for my mother, the family financier, to appropriate. There'd be a ten, a five, three ones, and some coins. Of course, money was worth more then. You could buy hamburger for nine cents a pound and butter for eight.

My father was born in Ripton, Vermont, in 1890, the son of Wallace and Ada Jane Billings and the only boy among five girls, one of whom died in infancy. Ripton, of course, is famous as the summer home of the poet Robert Frost. My dad joined the U.S. Army Signal Corps in World War I and was stationed in Manhattan, serving as a dispatcher in the medical division. Most people are unaware that army aviation was part of the Signal Corps until 1918 when it became the Army Air Service.

His job was to run emergency medicine from one New York City hospital to another. At that time and for military purposes, Manhattan traffic lights could be controlled on the main avenues to shut down traffic in order to allow the dispatcher safe and clear passage. Dad told me he would fly up Eighth Avenue, or wherever else he was sent on his Indian motorcycle, driving well over 100 mph to make his critical deliveries. In 1918, he was on one of those trips when a woman driving a Cadillac and obviously tipsy ran the red light and collided with my father.

When the ambulance came, the medical workers saw his body in a bloody jumble, and, shaking their heads, declared it was "too late." He had over a hundred broken bones. But he lived and even finished his service at the end of the war. As a young boy, I went with him once or twice to Chelsea Naval Hospital for treatment. My poor father. He stayed in constant pain for the rest of his life. This may explain why he kept a bottle hidden in his toolbox in the garage and away from my mother's teetotaler eyes. The fact that he completed his stint in the Signal Corps despite all odds set a powerful example before me. When Dad took up a task, he might not get it done in time but he always *would* get it done, like the time he saved the horses.

I was only two, but I can still picture my father, my uncle, and a barn in flames. We'd been visiting the aunts in Vermont, and on the way home to Scituate a huge fire came leaping into view. Even now I can picture Dad and Uncle Harry running through the front barn door and coming back out with horses. Immediately after, the whole front of the building was swallowed in flames and started pitching toward us. Fortunately, we were at a safe distance in my uncle's car. Dad wasn't afraid to face danger, and I've got to say that's in my genes too, just like the love of flying he imparted to me.

To feed our mutual appetite for aviation, Dad would drive us to all the local regional airports where we thrilled to hear the engines growling. His friend, Stafford Short, was the pilot of Boston and Maine Airways, which later became Northeast Airlines after the government forced the divestiture of any airline owned by a railroad. Boston and Maine had one Lockheed Electra, and on weekdays, Short flew it between Boston and Montreal. That was the airline's total schedule.

Sometimes Dad would take me with him over to Logan Field to watch Mr. Short land the evening flight. After all the passengers were off the plane, he would put me in the co-pilot's seat and taxi to the hangar for the overnight. I would ask questions, and he would answer them matter-of-factly, as if I were an adult and not a child who had yet to start first grade.

For my fifteenth birthday, Dad took me back to the airfield in Hingham for my first flying lesson. The plane was a Taylor Cub, a mono-wing tail-dragger with thirty-six horsepower and no brakes. The only way to steer it was to give it a blast on the engine while simultaneously pushing the rudder from side to side. To slow down you pulled the throttle back. Then you pulled the stick back, adding downward pressure to the tail-dragger's skid. This action served as a brake, similar to a foot slowing down a bike by scraping the sidewalk.

My lesson lasted about a half an hour and cost four dollars. The pilot took off, got off the ground, then said, "Here, make the airplane go." I made it go. It was exhilarating. I liked his teaching style and understood almost immediately what needed to be done. Even today I use his techniques. But after that there were no more lessons because there was no more money to pay for them.

Dad was handsome, jovial, and easy going. A heavy man, he had brown hair and was around five feet seven. He died of heart failure, too young at sixty-five. When he and my mother married, they moved to a rental unit in Scituate where he started building us a house on Stockbridge Road. Mom became pregnant with me. In her ninth month, she and Dad decided to visit her parents, and I decided to come. William and Blanche Bennett lived in Winchester, Massachusetts, right across from the hospital, and that's where I was born, in 1923.

Two weeks later we returned to the rental apartment and stayed until the house was finished. I was eight months old when we moved in. It was a single-story house with shake shingles, two bedrooms, a basement, and a square, enclosed porch centered on the street side. I've always felt proud of Dad for building such a fine home for his family. My sister Barbara came along in 1927, and as the house took on years, it brimmed with laughter and talk around the table, arguments and illnesses, the dreams and disappointments of family life. I hardly knew my brother, Bruce, who was born seventeen years after me and still lives in that house.

For years, my father thought he was a Scot and my mother, English. When I was five or six, a man in a suit came to our house and sat down at the kitchen table to interview Dad. He asked a great many questions and left, then returned a couple of weeks later with a beautifully drawn tree with names in it. "This is our family tree," Dad explained to us as he proudly displayed the picture. "It goes back to Robert Bruce, King of Scotland." He pointed out other important ancestors such as Josh Billings, an American author and humorist of the early nineteenth century. William Billings, the famous American composer, was also one of ours, he said.

Some eighty years later, I learned the truth of my father's lineage. Using a software program called Generations that included access to a genealogic database, I discovered that Alson Powers Billings came from Middle England and that his first known ancestor dated back to the year 800. He hadn't a single drop of Scottish blood in his veins! But Dad never knew it. The family tree sold to him so many years before was absolute fiction. That man at our kitchen table was smart. He knew he'd get money if he put down what my father wanted to hear. Further Internet searches revealed that Josh Billings was the pen name of Henry Wheeler Shaw. As for William Billings the composer, I couldn't make any connection with my father's line. Of course, if you go back far enough, you will see we're all related.

When I was seven, Dad decided we needed a boat and that he would build it. After all, he was a millwright and woodworker, and he'd built our house. "I'm going to need someone to help me," he said, and so I did my part, which meant I got to bring him a box of screws or a bottle of glue. The finished boat was a skiff twelve feet long. It had a square back and a pointy nose. The engine consisted of two oars that fit in brackets on each side of the boat. The waterproof plywood bottom was a recent innovation of the time. I was allowed to take the boat out to go fishing and given only one requirement: "Don't go beyond the sight of land." If I was fishing for flounder, I stayed inside the harbor, but for cod, I'd have to go out into the Massachusetts Bay. You could see land from even as far as five miles offshore.

My mother was Enid Alisca Bennett. She was born in Brookline, Massachusetts, in 1899. Her father, William Bennett, was of English descent, and her mother, Blanche Monroe, was half Scottish. Grandfather was an architect specializing in hardware. He invented the master key system, but as an employee of Yale and Towne, Inc., in Boston, he never received a penny for his invention, nor any recognition whatsoever, because everything an employee did was for the company's benefit. My parents met when Alson was visiting Harry, his buddy and my mother's brother. Alson was instantly attracted to Enid's warm, friendly spirit and lustrous auburn hair. They married in 1922.

She was a good mother – affectionate, fun-loving, and hard-working. The cast iron stove in her kitchen never grew cold. She used to bake pies and cakes – all kinds of tasty things with that stove, including Boston beans every Saturday night. I don't know how she did it. The gauge on the oven door, which I can picture clearly to this day, gave three temperatures: cool, warm, and hot. She must have had what we pilots call Vernier vision!

Dinners at our house were animated. When Dad got a little tipsy he would get up and recite poetry or quips from his "relative," Josh Billings. In a loud voice he declaimed the only two lines I remember: "Oh, the boy stood on the burning deck/peeling potatoes by the peck!" When Dad got *very* tipsy, he sometimes recited risqué verses, which brought a frown to Mom's face and a loud, disapproving "Alson!"

On holidays the house grew noisy and hot with company and my mother's fragrant pies. We had a gateleg table (which I inherited) that was stored in the front of our living room and dragged into the middle for Thanksgiving, Christmas, and other special events. Everyone grabbed a chair from wherever they could find one. Fourth of July was a big deal. Uncle Harry would drive down from Winchester a couple of days in advance with a huge wooden box of fireworks – he was the biggest kid among us. To Mom's dismay he would set firecrackers off from under the garbage can. Sometimes when Harry came for a weekend visit, he brought – unannounced – a half-dozen or so of his friends to go boating or fishing. Fortunately, my parents were very hospitable, and no one minded being dislocated. I'd be put in the attic on a cot or on the floor somewhere, and those who couldn't find sleeping space indoors would sleep out in the yard.

Mom enjoyed playing cards with Dad and her friends in the neighborhood. She loved people, and I think that part of her scraped off on me. What I didn't inherit was her artistic gene. With pen and ink or pencil she drew precise and beautiful images of what she saw around her. Once, visiting my grandparents in Winchester, I found a notebook of her drawings. These were finely detailed pictures of leaves and blossoms. I did retain the love of classical music she instilled in me, beautiful works like Bach's "Air on G String" and Beethoven's *Fifth Symphony* that I heard at home and at my grandparents' house.

Records then were shellac and ran at 78 rpm. I'd save up from my after-school and Saturday job at the mill where my father worked, and for thirty-five cents could buy a ten-inch classical record that lasted three minutes. A twelve-inch record cost fifty cents and played for five minutes. If you wanted to buy an entire symphony like Beethoven's *Ninth*, you'd probably need an album of twelve-inch records – eight or nine of them. This was before automatic record changers were available, so I'd have to change them by hand, one platter at a time.

Mom played the piano, Dad the violin and bass drum. They insisted I take piano lessons, which I endured for five years. Given the choice, I would have much preferred the sandlot. When I was five, Mom enrolled me in "classical" dance lessons, i.e., ballet. Barbara took them, too. For two years I wore leotards, she got the tutu, and I'm the one who got teased. Radio was a source of lively entertainment for our family as it was for others at that time. As a small boy snuggled up beside my mother on the sofa, I'd listen wide-eyed to the Lone Ranger and Buck Rogers. We liked the orchestra music that aired on Sundays, especially Wayne King, known as the Waltz King.

Every afternoon at around 4:30 or 5:00, Mom would call Barbara and me to the front porch room for what she called Children's Hour. Late sunlight would settle on her hair and face as she asked about our day at school and what we were learning. When we were very young, she read adventure stories and fairy tales aloud. Looking out, we played a game of guessing which lights belonged to Dad's car driving home on Stockbridge Road.

Chapter 2

Scituate

Satuit. That's my hometown's true name, the Wampanoag Indian word for "Cold Brook" that refers to a stream flowing into the town's harbor. Scituate is the anglicized name that stuck. The town is midway between Boston and Plymouth on the South Shore, with weather so cold that whenever the waters of the Massachusetts and Cape Cod Bays went above fifty degrees, it made headlines on the front page of the *Boston Globe.* There was a saying that went around town: "Summer comes to Scituate on August 27 at 2 p.m. and ends at 4 p.m." Cold as it was, growing up there was an adventure in freedom not experienced by most children today. The sea was my playground, the woods and marshes my hunting grounds.

With a population of 550 (excluding the summer tourists who owned or rented seasonal cottages), everyone was my neighbor. I could walk all over town day and night in perfect safety. This wanderlust got me in trouble, though. As a small boy, I used to escape from the backyard and walk the three minutes' distance to the train depot. There, I'd get on the train headed for Boston, excited to be going on a brave adventure. Just when the town had vanished and trees were flying by, the conductor would find me with my face pressed against the glass. "You again!" He'd call the police station, which was next door to our house, and the nearest patrol would pick me up and return me home where a switch awaited me.

One of my favorite places to play was the woods beyond the neighbor's land – they let us use it for a garden. I would climb the maple tree and crawl way out on the end of the highest branch. That was the cockpit of my airplane. I'd climb above the clouds and fly over mountains and rivers and towns, sometimes avoiding enemy planes. In the summer, from pre-school age until my teens, I would be sent to my grandparents' house in Winchester, where I'd spend a month or so and sometimes the entire summer. Their house bordered the Fellsway, a public preserve with a reservoir where the town's water was stored. It was forested with pines and deciduous trees and had no particular trail one could follow. I would leave after breakfast for my kingdom in the woods and not get back until suppertime.

My architect grandfather designed their house on Highland Avenue, and being the explorer that I was, I never tired of prowling around, especially in the attic. To get to it, I'd have to go upstairs to Uncle Harry's bedroom. On either side of his headboard, situated against the wall, were two doors. The door on the right was the closet. The one on the left opened to a set of stairs leading to the attic. I'd climb the stairs and, upon opening the squeaky wooden door, would be greeted with a wall of hot, stale air. The first thing to see in the dim interior was the water closet, always fascinating to me as a boy. This was an open, lead-lined wooden tank full of water that was supplied by the household waterpipe. It had a float valve and a chain that went through an opening in the ceiling at a handy height to the commode in the bathroom below. To flush, you'd pull the knob at the end of the chain.

The attic was everything an attic should be – cobwebbed, crowded with boxes and forsaken trunks, silent as stillborn time. I was seven when I came across a dusty old bedroom bureau whose drawers held the usual clutter and found a whole package of letters that Uncle Harry had written to his sister, my mother. Excited and somewhat anxious over reading someone else's mail, I sat down on the floor with my back against the bureau and untied the string that bound the envelopes. I read letter after letter, written in Uncle Harry's fine script and describing his wartime adventures.

Like my father, he'd served in the Signal Corps, but in the aviation section. His duty was to observe the trenches over enemy territory from the backseat of a Spad. This is a French manufactured biplane flown in World War I used initially for reconnaissance and later for fighting. In combat the pilot would actually fire a rifle or handgun right out of the cockpit. The Germans clearly had the upper hand here, mounting their machine guns on top of the cowling and synchronizing them with the propeller. The French and English, on the other hand, had to reach up and fire guns mounted on top of the wing. Some pilots would even stand up for better aim!

People adapt to technology as they find it, and it was no different for Uncle Harry. Due to limited space inside the plane, the key for Morse code was attached to the outside. My uncle would put his hand out to dot and dash back what he'd observed in the German trenches. In one letter, he wrote that the pilot of the day was Captain Eddie Rickenbacker (whom I too would someday meet). I could have spent hours reading, but I was a little boy with a tender conscience and worried that I was stealing by looking at those letters, so I put them back in the drawer and never saw them again.

SCITUATE

I liked hanging out with my hero, Uncle Harry. He was tall – around six-two – and had a long jaw. He also had the kindness to treat me like his best buddy. After graduating from Tufts University, he had become a master electrician and contracted for numerous jobs with the Winchester city government. "Come along with me, John," he'd say, and we'd ride in his Pierce Arrow convertible to various jobs in town. I wouldn't be an observer for long. Even though I was a little kid, he put me to work wiring outlets and switches and performing other such tasks.

One of his big projects was installation of the town's traffic control signal system, designed to be run either manually or automatically from a central location. Back then, traffic lights didn't have vehicle sensors; instead, the police controlled them with a timing device. Operations took place in an enclosed, elevated platform known as Five Corners that spanned Winchester's main intersection and was located next to the railroad station.

"You're gonna like this place," Uncle Harry said, motioning for me to follow him up one of the stairways that led from the sidewalk from either side of the intersection to the platform. The building was narrow – probably no more than eight feet across – and reminded me of a railroad car with windows. Two police officers were sitting on each side, facing in opposite directions and operating all kinds of switches in the system my own Uncle Harry had installed. I told him the place looked like a spaceship.

All the municipal employees knew him. We'd often drop by the firehouse and police station for a visit. The men would sit and chat over a smoke and a Coca-Cola, and I felt proud to be among them. Sometimes I'd go with Uncle Harry to Boston, where he had jobs as the supervising electrician for installing elevators in high rises. He'd take me up to the top of the tower where the relays were located to control the elevator system. I was awed by these mechanical wonders. I was awed by my uncle's towering abilities.

Like other families in Scituate, ours was rocked by the Depression. Work at the mill was slow and some days the only sound there was my father's pen, scratching on paper to check and recheck the bleak figures. At one point he was out of work entirely. How relieved he was when a local homeowner in town hired him to operate his personal woodworking shop. Unlike a professional shop, there were no safety devices. This certainly put Dad at risk, especially the time the bandsaw was running and the blade jumped off the follower, or upper wheel – it had most likely gotten out of alignment – and flew over his back while the driving wheel was still turning the blade. He quick-grabbed both sides of the blade encircling him and relieved the tension off the driving wheel below. For over an hour he held

9

that blade and didn't let go, for if he had done so, he would have been sliced in half. Finally, the shop owner returned and switched off the machine. All my father got were a few small cuts on his hand.

A source of relief for our town during those years of living hand to mouth was a freight train that came occasionally and dropped off a car at the railroad station. After its arrival was announced, everyone would show up to get a bag of potatoes or flour, whatever the government sent. These surplus items, bought by the Department of Agriculture from farmers to keep them from going under, were distributed all over the country. There was no red tape involved, no papers to be filled out. We needed food, and it came.

I had a few of my own ideas as to how I could help out. Flounders were plentiful in the Scituate harbor, but they wouldn't take bait except after they'd finished feeding at ebb tide. I found out that you could drop a sinker right on top of them and they would hardly move – if they did move a little, they'd soon go back to sleep. So, I devised a system. I bought a lead weight from the hardware store. Back then, such weights were used in windows that opened and closed with pulleys and were very inexpensive. I also bought a codfish hook and put it in a vise to straighten it out. These hooks are quite large. Now I had myself a barbed spear. I drilled a hole in both ends of the lead weight and put a screw eye in one hole for the line and the straightened-out cod hook in the other. Then I took the skiff out to the harbor where I drifted over the nest with my cod line, dropped it on the flounder, and pulled him on board. I'd come back with half a bushel of flounders. Maybe it wasn't the most sportsmanlike fishing, but the catch was always welcome at home.

On my ninth birthday, Dad gave me a .22 rifle, and I figured I could add variety to the table by bagging coots. I bought low-powered cartridges called CB caps that made hardly any noise when fired. In the predawn light, I would walk two miles to reach the marshes. There, I'd creep into the hummocks of grasses, hunker down, and wait for the birds to come for breakfast. Also called mud hens, the coots would feed in the tidewater pools. I'd lie prone in the grass, take a bead on the coot, and shoot him in the head, which would then drop into the water. None of the other coots noticed, however, because this is exactly what *they* did to get food – that is, put their heads in the water to gobble up small fish, snails, vegetation, and so forth. I'd shoot two or three birds and bring them home for supper – not my mother's favorite dish. If you like fish and duck, combine the two and that's what coot tastes like.

SCITUATE

When I was nine, my grandfather Bennett died and was laid out for days in an open coffin in the front room of my grandparents' house. Everyone but me was in the dining room eating. Looking at his still form – his hair neatly combed, his necktie perfectly knotted as it always was – I theorized, "He's probably just sleeping. Why doesn't someone wake him up?" After thinking about it for a while, I decided that *I* would be the one to wake him up, so I pried open one of his eyelids and said to myself, "Wake up and get out of that box, Grandpa." As if they'd heard my thoughts, the whole household suddenly piled in on top of me. My logic, always the better part of my brain, had failed me entirely.

My grandmother continued to live in the house until a few years later, when Uncle Harry got married and moved with his wife into a house of his own. It was too much for Grandmother to manage, so she came to Scituate to live with us until her death.

Chapter 3

Flying on My Mind

A block and a half away from our house was the Jenkins Elementary School. It was a typical, old-fashioned school with four big rooms on the first and second floors for classes. I can still see the gleam of the polished wooden floors and smell the smooth wax. There was also a cathedral-type attic set up as a theater and, believe it or not, served as the "office" of a dentist who came once a week to fill cavities or clean the teeth of Scituate children. His drill, operated with a pedal, worked somewhat like an old sewing machine. The pedal drove a big wheel and a leather belt that in turn would descend to an articulating arm and drive the drill with its deafening ...*Rrrrrr! Rrrrrr! Rrrrrr!*. There was no Novocain, no painkiller of any kind, so kids had unimaginable fun in that dentist's chair.

School was unimportant to me. By the time I started the first grade (we didn't have kindergarten), aviation was so thoroughly inside me that unless I had a piece of paper to draw airplanes on, well, I basically ignored my lessons. I liked looking out the window, daydreaming, imagining myself flying in a plane, then sitting on an asteroid looking down at the world. I especially admired seaplanes, those big flying boats that flew to the Orient. I'd be drawing intently when suddenly I'd hear a big whack of a ruler on her desk as Mrs. Dowd yelled, "JOHN BILLINGS! You get back in this classroom right now!"

I started making model airplanes when I was five. For a nickel, you could buy a small balsa glider kit with an engine called a rubber band. The plane had a wing that slipped into a slot on a stick with the rubber band. You'd furiously wind the propeller backwards and presto! – off the plane would go. Over the years, my model planes grew more sophisticated, and as I got better at it, I started building real models of existing airplanes. The skeleton of these was balsa, and we used what we called Japanese rice paper as the outer surface. If desired we could paint them, but I never bothered with that. I wasn't good at painting, and besides, I never built a model airplane to look at. I wanted to see them fly.

The next step was to glue the rice paper to the frame and sprinkle it with water. I used my mother's ironing mister to evenly wet the surface and shrink the paper so it would fit tightly over the plane. I was content with these projects until the day my best friend, George Williams, bought a small, single-cylinder engine that was fueled by methanol. His father had bought not only the engine but the whole expensive kit. George and I went to work, building the fuselage, wings, and other parts. Finally, the moment came for mounting the engine, which George did with utmost precision and care. Neither he nor I could contain our excitement. This bird was going to fly!

Early the next morning, I met George at his house and we walked to the beach. It was low tide and the sand was firm, perfect for take-off and landing. The sun was just beginning to appear over the horizon, shedding gold against the violet sky. There was plenty of space for our venture and scarcely a breath of wind. George propped the engine, adjusted the throttle for full power, and let it go. What a beautiful sight to see that plane climbing one, two, three – all the way to ten feet, then making a slow bank to the east. Wide-eyed, we watched it level out and keep going east. And keep going. Before long it had completely vanished, but we could still hear it faintly buzzing until it ran out of fuel.

That was the end of my own plan to buy an engine. I'd intended to save up money from a paper route I had (it paid one cent per delivery) to buy a motor at the steep cost of twenty-five dollars. But without the ability to remotely control the model plane, the plan was futile. At the time, no such device was available. Naturally, I went to Uncle Harry, who was visiting at our house for the weekend.

"Is there any way we could have controlled that model plane from the ground?" I asked.

After a long silence he said, "Yes, but you'll have to build it yourself. It's going to be a big airplane because it's going to be heavy." (Back then, tube technology was all that was available in electronics.) "There are no designs for it. You'll have to design it yourself."

I understood basic wiring – Uncle Harry had taught me about that before I'd even started school. But radio? Electronics? I knew nothing about them. "What should I do?" I asked him.

"Here," he said, and handed me a book called *Introductory Electronics*. I was thirteen and good at math. I read the book, understood it, and gave it back. He loaned me the next book, *Fundamentals of AC Circuitry*. Radio waves are alternating, so I needed to learn all about that type of current. I hadn't gotten far in the book when I came across something called a sine –

the sine of this and the sine of that. So, I wrote Uncle Harry a letter asking about it, and he wrote back, explaining that trigonometry was the kind of math referred to in the book.

I wasted no time walking to the town library near our house to check out *First Year Trigonometry: Plane and Spherical.* I asked the librarian if I could keep the book longer than the one-week due date, and she agreed – as long as I returned it if anyone else requested it. Fortunately, no one did. I kept it the whole summer.

I entered the ninth grade that year, and to my pleasant surprise, one of the classes was first-year trigonometry. Naturally, I took it and breezed right through the first lessons. On Friday of that first week of school, the teacher says, "John, do you mind staying? I'd like to talk to you afterwards."

"Okay," I said, wondering what I'd done to get in trouble.

At the end of the school day, I walked back to Mr. Gillespie's classroom, where he was working at his desk. Mr. Gillespie was an exceptional teacher and had a doctorate in mathematics. "So, what's this about trigonometry?" he asked, looking up from his papers. "Were you doing something with it this summer?"

I explained about the book I'd studied and how I'd worked the problems.

"Very good. There's something I'd like you to do for me." He opened his desk drawer and brought out a stapled set of papers.

"Sure. What is it?"

"Would you fill out this test?"

I agreed, and he handed me the test. I sat down at a desk and began working. It didn't take long to finish.

"Done already?" he asked as I returned the test. He graded it immediately, then looked at me with a big smile. "You got a ninety-eight. This is actually my final exam. Congratulations. You just passed trigonometry. So tell me, what other math would you like to take for the rest of the year?"

"Solid geometry," I said. Like all mathematics, I easily grasped and enjoyed this branch of it. The impetus behind all of these efforts, of course, was aviation and the radio-controlled model airplane I'd set my heart on building. I should mention that the math gene was strong on my father's side of the family. He told us a story about his sister, Hope, who as a fifth-grader was accused of cheating in math and got called in by the teacher.

"You must have the answers to these tests," her teacher said, "because nobody gets 100 percent on their work every single day."

"Go ahead and ask me some math problems now," Hope challenged. The teacher asked a couple of other teachers to join her in the evaluation. Hope readily answered every question they put to her.

FLYING ON MY MIND

"How did you come by those solutions?" the teacher asked.

"I don't know," was all she could say.

Hope's exceptional math abilities were reported to Middlebury College, and she was sent there for further evaluation. My father told us that she was given word problems only calculus could solve, but somehow Hope always had the answer. When she was asked how she did it, she'd say, "It was just there." She was completely unable to explain where the answers came from. My aunt never did pursue math but went on to become a nurse at a sanitorium in New York on top of one of the Finger Lakes mountains.

As I delved deeper into numbers, I decided that I wanted to steer toward pure mathematics as a career. I announced my intention at the Cipher Club. This was an informal group of math students Mr. Gillespie had organized to challenge his students with exercises in code and logic. Once a week we would come to his house after supper (actually, it was a rental apartment over a garage, but there was room enough for the handful of us "nerds").

Typically, Mr. Gillespie would say, "Okay, John, you write a message to Ralph. First you invent a cipher – any kind you want – and code it. Tear up the cipher and send him the message. And Ralph," he would say, turning to one of the other boys, "I want you to ferret out what he said."

It was during one of those cipher games that I announced my plan to become a mathematician. "And what kind of job do you think you're going to get with pure math?" Mr. Gillespie asked. "Look at me – I'm pure math." He abruptly disappeared and came back with an envelope in hand. "Here," he said to me. "Go ahead, open it." Inside was the check stub for his teacher's pay – scarcely more than what my father made as a millwright. "You'll want to become an engineer – math and electronics go together. But math alone won't get you anywhere."

This was but one of many instances when I was redirected toward my destiny of flying. My father certainly believed it to be so and didn't permit me to join sports teams in school.

"You could get injured and not be able to fly," he said. I ran track instead with his full approval and was pretty good at it. I could run a five-mile obstacle course around town and sprint to finish the last half mile in one lap. But he was unsuccessful in keeping me from joining my friends for ice hockey, a game we played as soon as winter came and the ice thickened on Hunter's pond.

We had no referee – it was strictly "ad hoc." I was thirteen, a big kid and welcomed by the others – not because I was good at aiming but because I was five-eleven, and it was hard to knock me down.

One frosty night we met for a game at the pond despite the rough surface. During the day, the ice had softened a bit and someone had walked across the pond, leaving footprints that refroze at night. Suddenly, as the sticks and insults were flying, some little kid pushed a two-by-four across the ice in my direction. I never saw it coming. It came scudding between my skates and down I went, striking my knee on a jagged ridge of ice. Though it hurt like hell, I jumped up and finished the game, thinking, "Errrr, just tough it out!"

We won that game, but I paid the price. When I got home I peeled off all my layers of clothing, overalls first, then two pairs of pants and down to my long underwear. It was soaked in blood. Mom came into my room, took one look, and called Dad. They went to work with scissors and picks to extract pieces of cloth from my wound, then called Dr. Handy, the town physician. He lived nearby and, like many doctors of the time, ran his medical practice from home. He came right over, cocked the lampshade by the bed for better light, and examined me carefully. "You know, there's a big hole right here." He showed my parents the huge gash, and I looked too, wincing in pain. "Your kneecap is broken in three places, young man. You're not going to be doing much skating for a while."

He took out what he called a wick and inserted it into the middle of the wound, then poured iodine all over it. Man, did it hurt! I put my hand over my mouth to keep from hollering. The next day Dr. Handy came back and the day after that for many days, pulling out the wick and putting in a new one each time. At one point, he began efforts to gently work the broken parts of my kneecap back into alignment. Finally, he exclaimed, "Ah! There it is!" The kneecap had healed and the pieces all matched up.

"Why didn't you stitch it up?" Mom asked.

"You've got to let it bleed out," he said. "If you stitch it up, germs and minute debris can stay trapped inside."

Not only did the fracture heal, the scar on my knee was minimal. This turned out to be a very fortunate circumstance, for when I had to undergo a physical to join the army, the doctor examining me said, "Hmmm, what a bad scrape. How'd you get the scar?"

"I fell on the ice," I told him.

"Boy, oh boy, are you lucky! You could have broken your kneecap."

"Oh?"

"If you'd broken your kneecap you wouldn't be here now."

Chapter 4

Earning My Wings

"A fighter pilot is a combination of a mathematician and an athlete, a scientist and a sharpshooter. He's got to know what goes on inside his plane. The heart of his fighter is steel and copper; its bloodstream is gas and oil. But its brain is the man who flies it."

– Captain Ronald Reagan
Wings for This Man

It's a cold December day, and I'm sitting on my workbench in the basement fixing a radio. My friend George Williams is helping me test the capacitors to make sure they're properly shunting AC to have a steady DC voltage at the output. I turn the knob and the radio starts humming. Just as I give George a nod, the hum turns into a voice.

"Damn them!" George says.

"What did they say?"

"They bombed Pearl Harbor!"

At that moment, I had no idea where Pearl Harbor was but I soon found out. An uncle of mine once removed was stationed at Wheeler Army Airfield in Honolulu, too close to Pearl for comfort. Thank God, the base wasn't hit, but I still knew what I had to do. A draft had been initiated. With all the other eligible Scituate boys, I had to go down to the post office and register. But I decided then and there I wasn't about to stand around and be drafted. Most likely I'd end up as an infantryman shooting someone right in my sights. I'd watched a few newsreels and heard horror stories from an older boy on leave from the infantry. I hadn't the stomach for that sort of warfare.

The only thing for me to do was enlist. Without telling my parents, I hopped on a train for Boston to join the U.S. Army Air Forces, or USAAF. It was June 1942, and I was almost nineteen.

"Is there a possibility I can get into flying?" I asked the recruiter. "I want to be in the aviation cadet program."

"Absolutely! No question about it," he said, with a big, encouraging grin. Later, I realized he was telling me what I wanted to hear so I'd sign my name.

When I returned home and told my parents I'd enlisted, Dad was pleased. Uncle Harry, who was visiting as he often did, was pleased. Mom was not. She'd seen what World War I had done to men and their families. "I'm not about to sign a permission slip so my son can go and get himself killed," she said with much heat. Actually, I needed only one parent's signature to make it official, and Dad, of course, readily signed. I hated to disappoint my mother, but I saw my chance to fly and nothing was going to stop me.

A few weeks later, I went back to Boston for my physical (that's when the doctor said it was lucky I hadn't broken my kneecap). "Billings, the army doesn't need to see you again until after you graduate," said the clerk as he stamped my papers. Back home, life resumed as usual. I went to school every day, worked at the lumber mill afterwards, and tried to hold at bay my visions of being a heroic war pilot.

Then one December morning – December 1 to be exact – as I'm sitting in history class, I see Mom standing in the doorway. The teacher approaches her and asks politely, "How can I help you, Mrs. Billings?" They speak in hushed voices, then Mom waves me over.

"You've been called to active duty and you're due in Boston at 6:00 a.m. tomorrow. They said you're to be at the railroad's South Station." She shakes her head in worry. "I don't know what we're going to do."

It was still dark when my dad drove me in our big Plymouth to the station in Boston. "Keep your nose clean," he said, slapping me affectionately on the back as he said goodbye.

The train was loaded with would-be soldiers. "Where are we going?" we asked each other, all of us fresh-faced and eager for adventure.

A voice from somewhere in the back of the car said, "You'll find out."

Several hours later, the train pulled into Atlantic City, and my life as a civilian came to an end. Boot camp was held at Camp Boardwalk. In 1942, the resort town's boardwalk and hotels were appropriated by the military for combat training and preparation. We spent a month marching and performing drills and calisthenics in the cold and memorizing military ranks and commands. Despite the incessant marching and freezing wind blowing off the ocean, it wasn't all pain and suffering. My billet was in a luxury hotel. The master ballroom was our mess hall, and many of the big bands came, including Glen Miller, and played from the balcony.

Sometimes we were treated to entertainment at the convention center known as Boardwalk Hall. There we were swallowed up in a sea of sonic grandeur,* as a musical artist whose name I don't recall played exquisitely on the world's largest theater pipe organ. I can't find words to describe that spectacular thunder. The organ had 33,000 pipes with blower motors totaling 500 horsepower! It seemed no time had passed before I was swept into the next phase of military life, bringing me closer to my dream of flying.

Someone in the army's upper hierarchy had decided it would be beneficial for prospective aviation cadets who'd never been to college to attend one. I was chosen for that group. Syracuse College was running a special ancillary program that included ten hours of flying time in a Taylor Cub, the plane I had flown for my fifteenth birthday. It was mid-January by now, and about a hundred of us from boot camp boarded a train for Syracuse. We arrived in a blizzard and marched from the station in the howling white wind to the campus where I would spend the next three months. I breezed through the required classes in math, history, and physics.

As one of only a few male students who hadn't yet gone off to war, I resisted the flirtations of the many attractive women on campus being as how my girlfriend, Nancy, was waiting for me back home. The best part, of course, was the time spent flying. Years later, I learned that the length of time spent in these classes was determined by the grades a student earned. I completed my stay in ninety days with a quarter of the original group.

After Syracuse, I left the North and took a train to San Antonio where I was assigned to the Aviation Cadet Classification (ACC) Center. It was May 1943. Obviously, I couldn't be in Scituate for my high school graduation, but

---

* *"The sonic Mt. Rushmore," as it's called by the internationally famous organist Steven Ball, is currently being restored. Ball is directing that effort and hopes to have the extensive project completed by 2023. If you're in Atlantic City you can see this massive organ, but only if you sign up for a tour. While you're there, you can also see two plaques recognizing Camp Boardwalk. The first reads, "In commemoration of Atlantic City's finest hour . . . Dedicated to the thousands of men and women of the United States Armed Forces who trained, served and recovered here from their wounds of battle during World War II – and to the devoted citizens of Atlantic City and Atlantic County who served and helped to make them feel at home." The second plaque commemorates the site of the Thomas England General Hospital – formerly Haddon Hall Hotel – and the largest U.S. hospital during World War II.*

I had all the credits I needed and was able to graduate in absentia. I even had a GI photograph taken of me in uniform which I sent back to be included in the yearbook. Meanwhile, upon arrival at the ACC Center, my fellow cadets and I were greeted with an enormous American flag, row after row of marching soldiers, and a sprawling complex of unremarkable buildings. We were processed in and issued our equipment, then given every kind of test imaginable – physical tests, academic tests, hand-eye coordination tests. The inevitable marching was part of this phase, and a lot of it. To me, it was a waste of time.

One exercise was to climb up a twenty-foot tower and jump down into a sandpit. This was supposed to simulate what it would be like to hit the ground after parachuting out of a plane and free-falling for twenty feet. We learned to bend our knees and roll forward. In the army we always were required to wear a parachute, but that jump was the only training we got. Fortunately, I never needed to open a parachute – never got shot down. At the end of thirteen weeks each of us was classified as to our position in the USAAF: navigator, bombardier, or pilot. Somehow, I managed to be enrolled in pilot training.

Next, we packed up our stuff and marched across the street to another facility – the Aviation Cadet Preflight School. There, we faced thirteen more weeks of marching and more academics. The classes were in math, physics, and aerodynamics. We studied weather, the principles of navigation, and the budding radio range system for airways, which was irrelevant for combat pilots since we could go wherever we wanted or needed to go. A typical day would begin with calisthenics, followed by breakfast. Then we'd head to our classes, which varied on different days so things didn't get too boring.

At least once a week we went on twenty-mile hikes. Some of them were actually exciting because there would be periods of live fire, and we'd have to crawl under a hastily erected web barrier parallel to the ground. Similar to chicken wire, it was tacked to small posts and raised about eighteen inches. The sergeant in charge roared out a command: "DO NOT, DO NOT, DO NOT STAND UP!" It was an order to be obeyed no matter what. Later, we heard through the grapevine that a soldier crawling under the barrier came face to face with a snake. Terrified, he jumped to his feet, pushed up the wire, and got knocked down by a bullet. That was enough to make you stay down.

Our superiors made sure we got plenty of time off. Once a bunch of us cadets rented a convertible and drove to a swimming pool about ten miles away. I was the designated driver, but it isn't what you think. As it happened,

I was the only one with a driver's license. Another excursion was to the Sunken Gardens, an abandoned quarry outside the city that had pathways with fantastic floral displays. On the base, we had three good meals a day, and you could take all the food you wanted. Not everyone, however, thought hash on toast was good eating, and they had names for food I can't mention. But boy, you never left a crumb on your plate.

Then came the order we were all waiting for: "Pack your bags, men. Time for primary flight school." Training in the USAAF was conducted in three phases: primary, basic, and advanced. Each period lasted thirteen weeks. Our destination was Coleman, Texas, a small town in the central part of the state. This was in December 1943. The very best training that a person who wants to fly happened to me, and I couldn't be more grateful. Coleman Field was activated in 1940 as one of dozens of contract primary flying schools and operated by the Austin Flying Service. The U.S. Army took over everything, including the instructors. The only military pilots we came across were those who would be doing our check rides. Flying was all stick and rudder, with few instruments. If you got inside the clouds, there was nothing to assist you. The best thing you could do is simply let go. After all, the airplane knows how to fly.

Training was in a PT-19, a low-wing, open cockpit monoplane built by Fairchild that had 180 horsepower, no electricity – not even a battery – and an inertial flywheel that had to be hand cranked, just like in the Curtiss Robin of my first flight. I'd get the airplane ready, and another cadet would come over. When I gave him the signal, he'd plug a crank into the side of the airplane and crank up the flywheel. Then he'd pull the crank out and yell, "Contact!" and everyone would scatter.

We learned basic flight maneuvers: straight-and-level, turns, climbs, and descents. One day, unexpectedly, my instructor climbed out of the plane and said, "Now you take it around." My first solo flight! I took off and made a landing. This was the ultimate, the sky's blue flame and my lifelong passion. I'd been told to look over to where the instructor was sitting in the grass. He would wave me on if he wanted me to do it again, and happily, he did. I made my second circuit of the pattern, thrilled to be flying all by myself and enjoying every second. When I looked over, he signaled to me, so I taxied over. "You're doing good," he said, "except why don't you try it one time with the flaps up?" I felt like an ant under an elephant's foot.

After thirteen weeks of primary training and sixty-five hours under my belt as a pilot, we went to Majors Field in Greenville, Texas, for basic training. There we got instrument and radio training, night flying, flying in

21

formation, aerobatic maneuvers, and a lot of laughs from Bob Hope when the USO came to town. The trainer, manufactured for the USAAF by Vultee Aircraft, was a BT-13 Valiant, otherwise known as the Vultee Vibrator. It was a two-seater with a big 450 horsepower engine, a canopy over the seats, and an electric system. You just pushed a button to start it. Boy, it felt good!

Right off the bat we were taught an unusual landing pattern that became commonplace. If you were finished for the day, you'd go over the runway (not a grassy field like the primary, but a real runway) at 2,000 feet above ground level. On the upwind leg, you'd look to your right to see who was there, and if there was a space, you'd roll over on your back and split S into the downwind leg. These and other aerobatic maneuvers like lazy eights and chandelles were great fun – sometimes your chin would touch your belly button! For instrument training, we flew "under the hood." A black hood was pulled up over the pilot's position in the cockpit and fastened, forcing us to rely entirely on our instruments. The instructor would be in the back cockpit looking out for traffic and on alert to handle anything that went wrong.

After basic, we were sent to the little town of Frederick in southwest Oklahoma for advanced training. This was in a twin-engine airplane made by Cessna, the UC-78, otherwise known as the Bamboo Bomber because of its wood and fabric construction. The U was for utility because the military used it, not only for training pilots, but navigators and bombardiers, too.

One night a student and his instructor were flying, when suddenly the engine caught fire. "Abandon!" yelled the instructor. "If you slow down, you're going to get stepped on." So they went to the back (unlike other airplanes, the door was near the back and opened over the wing) and jumped. The fire burned itself out and the airplane kept flying until it ran out of fuel and landed, lethally damaged and unflyable. Its left wing was found with gaping holes from where the instructor and student had smashed through the wooden ribs to escape. This was the plane that transitioned us to combat flying!

On March 8, 1944, I got my wings and a shiny gold bar that commissioned me as a second lieutenant. I don't recall a single member of our class of 300 washing out. We'd all come through the rigors of training – countless hours of study and flying practice – and now we were junior officers in the USAAF. It was quite a day, topped off with a thirty-day leave. The commissioning ceremony was held in one of the large hangars. Long tables were set up with many neat stacks of paper. One of the soldiers in charge said, "Fill out this form. If you're not going home for leave, then put down the address where we can get to you because your orders will be sent there."

We also had to write down what we wanted to do in combat. I thought to myself, *Well, since I can't be a fighter pilot right now, I guess I'm destined to fly a bomber.* So I put down that I wanted to be an A-20 pilot. The A-20 Havoc was a twin-engine light bomber made by Douglas for a two-man crew and used for close ground action by the Brits and French as well as the Americans. Then I took my seat in the bleachers. The soldier in charge stood in the middle of the hangar and said loudly, "You know, I've been looking at these wishes of you guys, and I can't see a single one that you won't get!" Well, that made my day.

Afterwards, I took a train home, excited to be going to see my family and eager to show off my new dress uniform. Mom greeted me at the door. When she saw my wings and butter bar, she threw her arms around me. "John, look at you! So handsome! And to think you're a pilot!" she cried, a beaming convert from her previous disapproval of my military career. Dad was clearly proud. After all, his son was fulfilling his own dream of flying.

I, too, had considerable pride in what I was doing, and I suspect it showed. I was grateful for the opportunity to serve my country and to do so as a pilot. It was good to be back in Scituate, to share my adventures with everyone, and hang out with what school chums were still around. But inwardly I was itching to get back into the cockpit. In fact, my life's motto was formed then and there: "The time the soles of your feet aren't touching the ground doesn't count!"

Chapter 5

Getting Personal with the Pig

I looked as far as I could see across the long concrete apron of the Liberal Army Airfield to find the A-20 I was supposed to fly. But all I saw were lineups of great big, ugly airplanes. Well, there weren't any A-20s, as I soon found out. I don't remember anyone asking me if I wanted to fly the "Pregnant Pig" known as the Consolidated B-24D Liberator.

We'd arrived at the B-24 Command Pilot Training Center in Liberal, Kansas, after four long days of travel on a troop train from Boston. Training was going to be comprehensive. The old program was seen as inadequate in preparing wartime pilots and had been scrapped.

"So, where's the curriculum?" the colonel appointed to develop the school said.

The general replied, "You're going to create it. We want these people to learn to fly under all conditions."

Under the previous training system, a new-minted pilot was sent overseas as soon as he got his wings and put in an airplane in the co-pilot's seat where he'd be taught by an experienced command pilot. But this arrangement could spell disaster in combat, especially on his first mission where the enemy might wipe out the pilot in command and make the inexperienced co-pilot take over the position. The new strategy was to teach the pilot everybody's job from scratch.

We were given an outline of our training schedule, which was – you guessed it! – for thirteen weeks. Six days a week would include eight hours of classroom, eight hours of flight training, eight hours of sleep, a half hour each for breakfast and lunch, and a whole hour for dinner. Chapel on Sunday was mandatory. The only free time we got was every other Sunday afternoon. I made a mental note to find time to refresh my basic arithmetic skills so I could figure out how I had been misled as to the number of hours in a day.

And so we learned to fly. There were three classes a day. One was in the B-24, with six trainees on board. Each student would log an hour in the left seat. The first take-off was completed with all four engines running, but all the rest were with one or more engines *failing* before lift-off. Sometimes, two engines on the same side would fail. We got so accustomed to those failures that when the instructor pulled only one throttle, it became a non-event.

Except for the first few times, the instructor didn't occupy the seat but sort of wandered around. I might be in the pilot's seat, student number two in the co-pilot's seat, student number three doing the navigation, student number four operating the radio. You learned everybody's job whether you would ever need to do it or not.

The second class was in a crashed plane outside the classroom building. Most of the outside skin had been stripped to allow us to see structures like wiring, hydraulic lines, cables controlling the surfaces, and others. We prowled through that plane and took it apart to learn what each thing was and what it did, from the cowl flaps to the compass housing and everything in-between.

The third was classroom training where we learned the various systems of the B-24: hydraulics, electrical, fuel, and the control cable system. Eventually we could draw a diagram of each one, which we had to do for our final exam. We studied aircraft and engine performance, weight and balance in a normal state and with parts missing. We studied navigation theory and weather patterns. The more we learned, the more our respect grew for the "Pregnant Pig."

As in every school, mishaps occur. One night, as the plane accelerated to fifty mph, the instructor pulled the throttle to the number one engine all the way back to idle. The runway was long enough that I could have easily retarded the other three engines to idle and stopped before running off the end. But that wasn't the drill. Just for practice, I was to continue as if it were a short runway. At about ninety, he pulled number two. Now both left-side engines were idling while the two right engines were on take-off power. This caused the plane to veer to the left. To keep it on the runway, I had to put both feet on the right rudder pedal and push as hard as I could and hold. I didn't have time to trim right.

The force sheared off the pin in the seat track, and I started sliding backward in my seat (it was made of heavy armored plate and called a coffin seat because it looked like we were sitting in a coffin). I thought, "Oh shit!" and instinctively reached with my right hand for the retarded throttles, but the instructor's left hand got there first. The seat continued to the end of the rail, breaking the end stop and landing on its back under the top turret with me still strapped into the 300-pound tub, wondering if the airplane was going to make it. We did make it, I escaped from the coffin and we got the rest of the night off.

The strange story of one man's survival took place on a Sunday afternoon when we had the luxury of a few hours off. I'd gone into Liberal with some buddies to watch a movie. We could hear loud rumblings of thunder outside. About midway through the film, the power suddenly went out. The manager pulled the chains to turn on the gas lights used back then, stepped up onto the stage, and addressed the audience. "Please, everyone, just sit still. These storms happen often, and we're very good about the power. It should come on soon and we'll finish the movie."

The power came back in about half an hour and we finished the movie. When we returned to the base, we found out that the thunderstorm had spawned a tornado that tromped right across the base and raised up a B-24, turning it completely over. It landed upside down on top of the airplane that had been next to it in line! The tornado struck our billets, too, and made matchsticks of three of them. The billets, not made to withstand storms, were typical two-story buildings with beds lined up along the walls and a single bathroom on each floor. The tornado struck two buildings in a row, skipped over one, and devastated the fourth. One of the guys had decided to take a nap that Sunday afternoon. He was on the bottom floor in the bottom bunk of a wrecked building and to everyone's amazement, never got a scratch. It did wake him up, though.

Sleep was hard indeed to come by. The intensity and long hours of training took a toll, and exhaustion worked its way deep into our bones. But it was never an excuse for staying on the ground. "You think you won't be fatigued on a mission turned bad?" the instructor would taunt. One student in squadron three decided he needed sleep more than dinner, so he set his alarm and grabbed a nap. He slept right through the bell, and when he woke up, he sprinted to the flight line, only to see his flight taxiing away. Remorseful, he went into the flight operations center and confessed.

"Just run over to squadron one – they had someone go on sick call," said the soldier in charge. He signaled a lineman to drive the student over to the airfield on a tug. But once again, it was too late. He watched with dismay as the airplane lifted off. "Go back to bed," they told him when he went back to report to operations.

Later that night, we learned those two B-24s had been doing instrument practice using low-frequency signals to navigate the Gage, Oklahoma, radio range. But somehow the planes failed to communicate with each other and collided nose to nose, engine to engine. No one survived. Parts of one plane were found jumbled up in the other. It was quite a thing to think of. I've always wondered about the student pilot who, like the man in the billet, cheated fate.

One mishap nearly sent me to the blue beyond, and I've never forgiven the instructor for what he did to me. It was a daylight training mission, and I had just finished my turn in the pilot's seat. It was time to train as a radio operator even though it was a job the combat pilot would never actually do.

"Okay, Billings, go get the frequency meter," the instructor said, "and tune up a new frequency for the long-range transmitter." I was to transmit a message back to the base in Morse code; they would send an answer. Now, pilots were supposed to carry their parachutes with them on every airplane excursion. We didn't wear parachutes, only the harnesses. The chute itself was stowed on the wall near the pilot's station and snapped onto the harness when needed. Since the meter was strapped down over the second bomb bay, I had to go through the whole catwalk and up over the top of both bays. The catwalk was only about eight inches wide. You dared not lose your balance because if you did, you would go straight through the lightweight, aluminum doors below that opened like a roll-top desk.

Carefully, I stepped past the first bay and was nearing the second when suddenly the whole floor opened underneath me and bright sunlight rushed up into the dark interior. Eight-thousand feet below was the world with its tiny houses and roads. The instructor had opened the bomb bay doors! Terrified, I grabbed the first stanchion and hugged it with all my might. When I looked over my shoulder, I saw the instructor – he was laughing! Then he closed the doors.

Though thoroughly shaken, I was determined to perform the task he'd assigned and managed to unbuckle the frequency meter. With the device in hand, I went to the back of the plane and climbed up over the wing. It was dark where I sat, all except for a little dancing light that poked through a missing rivet. That day in Kansas was a hot one, and the heat was adding to the B-24's gyrations as the instructor, sitting in the right seat, was now conducting unusual position training. The left-seat student was required to keep his head down during these godawful maneuvers, and then, looking only at instruments, he had to right the airplane.

As the plane rolled into a steep turn, I noticed that the spot of sunlight was dancing a little too exuberantly – and boy, did my stomach ever notice it too! I dropped the meter and ran toward the waist gun position, opened the large window for the side gun and leaned out, emptying the contents of my stomach to the vastness of southwest Kansas – oblivious to the fact that I could have fallen out and plummeted to my death. Two footnotes to that day: that was the only time I ever got airsick and the only time from then on that I failed to carry my parachute with me, even though I would never need it. This was due in large part to the rapport and skilled teamwork of my flight crew, whom I would soon meet for the final phase of my training and who would be with me throughout combat operations.

The newly created Flight Crew Coordination Training Center was in South Carolina at the Charleston Army Air Field, still in use today and still, as then, a dual use airport for both military and commercial aircraft. I arrived on June 21, 1944. Training was designed to build solidarity, trust, and teamwork among the crew members – ten in all – to make us a formidable aerial fighting force. It also gave us the opportunity to learn each man's strengths and weaknesses. I was a replacement pilot, and the men were dismayed at first since I had only one shiny gold bar and my predecessor had two silver ones. He was the old man, so to speak – in his upper twenties, a captain through and through. He had met misfortune at Charleston Beach while rough-housing with the men in the waves and wound up with two broken legs. I was only twenty but already possessed a leadership style of leading by example rather than by edict. To fill the old man's shoes, I had to do a lot of catching up, but it didn't take too long. Nor did it take long for our crew to bond.

We worked as a unit. We called each other by our first names. We billeted together. We depended on each other. It was this solidarity that would save our lives over and over. Though decades have passed and I'm the only crew member left, I carry the faces and stories of those men with me always. They were Roland Nix, co-pilot; Charles H. Smith ("Smitty"), navigator; Richard ("Dick") E. Gottleber, bombardier; Warren D. Eldridge, engineer; George Boyas, radio operator/gunner; Glen L. Sandberg, belly, or ball turret gunner; Jackson R. Baker, waist gunner; Lonnie V. Dunham, Jr., waist gunner; and William Davis, nose turret gunner. Actually, William Davis was a replacement for a crew member who suffered from airsickness and who wanted terribly to be the nose turret gunner, but his condition got so bad that even getting into the seat caused him to throw up!

Smitty was the new old man. He was married and already had a child under a year old. He actually wanted to be a navigator, which was unusual. Most navigators were wannabe pilots who didn't make the grade. But

Smitty had studied and decided the navigator was the most important person in the airplane, and at times he was. He was an addict when it came to calibrating instruments and getting things exact. The youngest was Glen, the ball turret gunner. He looked like an escapee from a middle school. After the crew had been together for a while, Glen asked to speak to me alone.

"There's something worrying me, John. I'm scared we might be doing a combat operation and I'm in the belly turret when a bullet strikes and damages it. Then I won't be able to get back into the plane and the turret won't retract because of the strike. And you'll have to land the plane with the turret extended and then it'll be ground to pieces with me inside it." I paused for a moment to take in his words and do some quick thinking. He looked at me expectantly.

"Don't worry. If that ever happens, I've got some ideas."

Not long afterward, we were on a training mission and Glen was down in the belly turret. To his dismay, the retractable mechanism malfunctioned and the turret wouldn't come up. Sandburg was able to open the small turret door and with the help of crew members, get out and into the plane. From the base command came the order, "Just come in and land. We'll put a new ball turret in."

"Okay," I replied. "As long as we're going to do something, let's try this. I'd like to have the whole runway, and I don't want any interference. What I do want is for you to chase the airplane on the ground. I'll maneuver to a stop that I think will elevate the rear end of the plane, then somebody will get out of the truck and put a bar under the tail and tell me when it's there. Then I'll shut the engines off."

So, I came in, but not real slow. I wanted to be very flat. I asked all the crew members to come up to the cockpit to make it nose-heavy. They came forward. I put the main wheels down and landed flat. I let the nosewheel hit, then started on the brakes. As you can imagine, if you apply the brakes hard, it makes the nose go down, and that's what happened. As the plane slowed nearly to a stop, I added power to the props – and power is what I had – a thousand horsepower in each engine. Sure enough, the guy got out of the truck, put a bar under the tail, and came around. I cut off the engine, and we all got out of the plane and left it in the middle of the runway, allowing about two inches of free space under the turret and pavement. I didn't leave a scratch! There was absolutely nothing I could do from that day on to disappoint my ball turret gunner.

From the Charleston airfield we flew dry runs to various destinations of our choice, such as the Caribbean, as long as they met the specified distance requirement. One day, Roland, my co-pilot, said he'd like to take a look at his hometown. "Do you think you could pick out the house?" I asked.

"Oh, yeah, sure."

We hatched a plan where Roland would write a note and we'd make a little parachute out of a handkerchief to fasten to it. "At your command, we'll have somebody throw it out the waist window," I suggested. As we approached the small town of Anniston, Alabama, I came down to an altitude of twenty feet, and the note was floated down.

At this point, I must digress momentarily because of the strange coincidence surrounding that note, and skip forward to 2001. My wife Barbara's sister had died and we went to the funeral in Charlotte, North Carolina, where Barbara had grown up. There, I met many of her relatives for the first time. So that night in our room I brought out a yellow legal pad and said to my wife, "I need some help here. Can you tell me who is who and what's the relation?" I wrote down everything she told me and finally got a sense of her family structure.

Back home, using my Generations software (the program that had exposed the fraud of the huckster who'd sold my father a family tree), I created Barbara's family tree. Before long I started receiving a firestorm of chat messages. A few were from a young lady who gave me leads on people in Barbara's genealogy. One day we happened to be on our computers at the same time and started chatting back and forth. At one point I asked her where in the world she lived, and she answered, "It's a little town in Alabama that you've never heard of – Anniston."

"Well," I wrote, "my co-pilot – Roland" – I stopped mid-finger on the Nix because it hadn't sunk in that the name I'd been seeing all along on her chats was such and such NIX!! And that's what I sent her - NIX, all caps.

She came right back and said, "If you had looked out the cockpit window that day when you flew the B-24 down Main Street, you'd have seen a little girl running and jumping over stone walls chasing the little parachute made out of a handkerchief. That note was from my Uncle Roland!" It's a small world indeed!

In the B-24 we did a lot of formation flying, night flying, and mock missions where we dropped 100-pound sand-filled bombs, each equipped with a detonator to release smoke on impact so we could see where we'd hit. We trained extensively as part of the CNT course – Celestial Navigation Training. A synthetic airplane known as a Link Trainer (named for Ed Link, its co-creator) had a cockpit that could accommodate a navigator, pilot, co-pilot, and radio operator or instructor. Roger Connor, an aeronautics writer for *National Geographic,* called it "a technical marvel that provided an excellent trainer for a broad range of equipment and procedures ranging from sextants to bombsights." We learned to navigate by the stars. This was accomplished by viewing "stars" that were actually lights mounted where real stars should be. All of this took place in a large building with a domed, planetarium-like ceiling.

The army had built a mile-long track before our arrival to be used for more than running. Trap machines were positioned along the track's outside perimeter, spaced thirty feet apart and operated by GIs who would launch clay pigeons for us to shoot. Our crew took turns in a turret mounted on a pickup truck with a shotgun we fired as the truck moved around the track at twenty-five mph. With the pigeons released from all directions, we benefited from this exceptional in-motion training that prepared us for enemy attacks. Not only would an enemy airplane be in motion, but we'd be in motion, too, and all of this had to be reckoned. Dick and I were gun nuts, so we thought of it as play more than training and considered the exercises great fun.

One day, all the flight crews on base were called to an assembly. The general stood in front, glaring at us. "Until somebody comes forward to admit to what they did, everyone's going to pay." We were accused of flying not just one but five B-24s under a high bridge at Charleston Beach at night. We looked at each other in disbelief. Nobody admitted it because nobody had done it. Nevertheless, we were put on disciplinary stand-down and prohibited from going to the canteen or taking any time off. Well, we soon found out that five B-17s from a base across the state were responsible. "Men, I apologize," the general said, and things went back to normal.

Time off frequently meant the beach. Dick and I would rent a boat and go fishing. Sometimes we had guests who came over to play with us – dolphins! Once, we caught a couple of sand sharks about two feet long. That night the cook made us a tasty dinner. One summer evening the whole crew went to the beach and stayed for a party hosted by the city for the public. Someone brought a wind-up record player. The ocean breezes caught the lively jazz music and the beach was hopping. There was dancing. There were girls. I figured the bodies of gals "cooked" better in the South than up North, and I was right. One girl in particular caught my eye – she was almost wearing a swimming suit. She was very voluptuous and carefully guarded by her father, who noticed the way I was eyeing her. "Look here," he said, pulling me aside. "She's only twelve, so don't get any ideas!"

On July 23, our unit left for Mitchel Field on Long Island. This was a staging area for B-24s and their crews. At last I was going to get my airplane! Or so I thought.

Chapter 6

On the Way to War

Our bomb crew rode in on a train to Mitchel Field like a pride of lions. We were eager to get into the action overseas, to do all we could to stop the Nazi menace. But the grim realities of war were on the far horizon of our experience. Our excitement mounted when three young ladies in flight suits arrived from Michigan to deliver what we thought was *our* B-24 (on arrival to Europe we found out otherwise).

The Women Airforce Service Pilots, or WASPs, had received the same aviation training as male cadets, only without combat and gunnery. The airplane came straight from Willow Run, the factory east of Ypsilanti built by the Ford Motor Company that at peak production turned out a B-24 every fifty-five minutes. It's well known that more B-24s were produced than any other bombers during the World War II era. The crew decided that I would name the plane, and so I called her Nancy Lee, after my sweetheart back home.

After we'd been in Long Island for about a week, we got our orders to go to Italy. The army had contracted with Pan American to provide a chief navigator for the trip, and we were given the flight coordinates. After picking up the plane, we did a couple of short flights to get our feel of it and check everything out.

At last, launch day arrived: August 21, 1944. Each crew member took his position. After a visual inspection of the plane, I unlocked the access door at eye height on the right side ahead of the bomb doors. Then I reached in, pulled the auxiliary bomb valves, and opened the doors. After a few other preliminaries, I climbed into the cockpit, started the engines, and taxied down to the end of the runway for the preflight check. Everything looked good. Time to launch! Mixture full rich, prop controls full forward, throttles full forward for take-off. We smelled the fuel, felt the vibrations.

An hour and a half later we arrived in Bangor, Maine, the jump-off point for the flight to Italy along the southern route. From there, it was 730 nautical miles to Gander, Newfoundland, where we stopped to refuel before heading for the Azores, then on to Morocco, Tunisia, and finally Italy.

"Sorry, fellows, we're shutting down the flow," the Pan Am navigator announced. "Weather in the Atlantic is rough. Heavy cloud cover at 15,000 feet. We're standing down." So, we spent five days in Gander, a little town in Newfoundland and the site of the world's largest airport at that time, which was the crucial staging point for ferrying military aircraft overseas. The temperature was mild in late summer in an otherwise frozen country, with blue skies, lakes, mountains – the perfect weather for Dick and I to head for the skeet field. We found out that the army would give us any amount of ammunition that we wanted to keep us happy, and for two guys who loved to shoot, this was happiness on a platter. I'd say we went through at least two cases of ammo during our stopover in Gander.

Late one night I was sitting in the airplane writing a letter home and listening to a local broadcast station with the APU running (that stands for auxiliary power unit, nicknamed "putt-putt"). Suddenly the order came down: "We're going to launch at 4:00 a.m." I managed a few hours of sleep, splashed water on my face, pulled on my flight suit, and prepared to go. We were one of about twenty airplanes in position, waiting to launch. As I made routine adjustments, I noticed the manifold pressure on engine number two running away. "What's with this?" I wondered.

Normally, electronics brings up the manifold pressure by closing off the wastegate. The wastegate is a valve that redirects exhaust gas away from the turbine and protects the engine and the turbo charger. On number two, the wastegate didn't open, and the manifold pressure kept increasing. I pulled number two's throttle, thinking it was just a surge and would come back. But it didn't. I knew I couldn't take off. There was plenty of room to stop, so I pulled all the throttles, taxied off the runway, and returned to the end of the line. This gave me time to recheck number two. It was steady. The only thing that didn't register normally was the cylinder head temperature, but I figured that it was okay since we were on the ground. Everything looked normal, so when our turn came to go, we launched. Time passed. Sunrise happened, rosy-blue with lavender streaks and the glint of new sun. The concerns I'd had on the runway had long vanished as we cruised over the vast Atlantic. Just as I was thinking how good my chocolate bar was going to taste, Warren, the engineer, came up to my position. "I think we have an oil leak in number two engine."

"Well, it's running pretty good now," I said. "All engine indicators are in the green. Just keep an eye on it." In the B-24, there was no separate gauge for oil quantity. I knew the oil pressure gauge would let me know if there was a leak.

Pretty soon after that, the navigator said, "Point of no return." This meant the Azores was the closest destination, and it was three hours away.

Five minutes later, Warren came back. "I checked again, and that rudder's getting black. We're definitely losing oil in number two."

I looked down – the instruments still appeared normal. "Well, look, everything's just . . ." At that moment, the red light came on and the oil pressure plunged. The co-pilot hit the red button for feather, a technique to rotate the propeller blades parallel to the airflow to reduce drag when there's engine failure. But I had confidence in the plane and the crew. We made it safely to the Azores and Lagens (now called Lajes) Airfield on the island of Terceira. I reported that number two engine was feathered.

"Roger," the air traffic controller said. "Circle the airport for a while. We're changing the runway direction. As soon as we get the mobile tower positioned, we'll call you."

Well, I didn't have an actual emergency, so I couldn't yell at him, though I was tempted to. I mean, we were exhausted, and our nerves were rattled. If it had been really critical I'd have said, "Get everybody off the runway, I'm coming in." But I didn't, of course. We circled. Finally, we were cleared to land. Turns out we got to spend a week in paradise while waiting for a new engine. What happened was this: the cylinder head had blown off. Being the only cylinder that transmitted the temperature to the cockpit, it wasn't hot, of course, and we had no way of detecting the problem.

The dazzling contrasts of the Azores – a group of nine volcanic islands under British occupation during the war – provided a refreshing interlude from military rigors. From the crystal-clear lakes to the black sand beaches and underground caverns, we absorbed the tranquil beauty surrounding us. Our favorite activity was swimming. We went out the first day for an ocean swim, but there was no beach, only volcanic rock rising six feet above the water. I looked down into the crystalline depths and pointed out to the men a rock down below that would impale them if they dove. While it was impossible to gauge distance due to the water's super clarity, I figured it would be safe to leap butt first, like cannonballs, to keep it fairly shallow. After splashing and horse-playing with the guys for a while, I decided I would swim down to the rocky bottom. Growing up in Scituate, I was a saltwater child and pretty good swimmer – I could easily surface dive twenty feet. I swam down and farther down until I started seeing spots. I figured I was deep enough but still no closer to the underwater rock, which in reality might have been more than thirty feet below. So, I headed back up to the surface and joined the others. After we finished swimming, we climbed back up to ground level and lay on the rock we'd jumped from, sunning ourselves on its flat face. "Hey, look at that," said Smitty. I looked down to see a massive shark gliding by the underwater rock I never reached. As I said, appearances are deceiving!

Another time, we were returning from a swim and noticed a tidal pool full of tiny fish. "Just watch," someone said. "Something's going on." We stood there observantly: one moment a swirl of movement, then the next, nothing. A little fish would simply vanish, poof! Just about then, an indigenous man from the island walked by. He greeted us in Portuguese, and we signaled for him to come over.

"Ah," he said, watching as more fish disappeared. He reached his hand down into the water, pulled out a small octopus, and carried it home.

Finally, we got our new engine and said goodbye to our island heaven. Our next stop was Marrakech. We arrived at around 3:00 in the afternoon and stood spellbound as we took in the crazy quilt of sounds and smells and swarms of people in exotic robes.

"Let's go to the Kasbah," Dick suggested. That's where all the drinking went on, but not for the locals, of course, because they were Muslims and Muslims don't drink. You could buy almost anything there, including ladies. "Hey, we can catch that truck!" Dick said.

In the distance we saw the jitney roaring from the Kasbah in a cloud of dust. But it didn't stop to pick us up at the bus stop. Instead it zoomed to the next stop, and with squealing brakes, stopped in front of the infirmary. We hurried over to see what was going on. An American soldier got off – a gunner from another crew – and he was covered in blood, with his hand draped in cloth that looked like someone's shirt.

"What happened?" I asked.

Grimacing in pain, he said, "I whistled at one of those ladies wearing a veil up to her nose, and a guy pulled out a machete and swung it at me. I put my hand up instinctively, and the thing cut all but one bone." He showed us how his hand flopped, like a fish. We looked at each other, bravely turned around, and made tracks back to our billet as fast as we could.

The next day we flew to Tunis, a trip of about four hours, spent the night, and headed for Gioia, Italy. Gioia del Colle Airfield was the primary maintenance base where all the new aircraft for the Fifteenth Air Force went, of which we were part. Then came the stunning order: "Take everything off the airplane because you'll never see it again." We were totally unprepared for the news that the B-24, which had safely carried us from America and across the Atlantic over many miles and hours, wasn't ours after all. So, we grabbed our B4 bags – these were a kind of fabric suitcase that folded in two and had two pockets on the side and a handle – and our parachute bags, which held the parachute and harness.

Then we walked across the airport and were about to cross the main runway we'd just landed on, when I yelled, "Hold up! Somebody's on final!" We stopped to look. But what were we looking at? "What kind of airplane is that?" I wondered. It kind of looked like a B-24, but something was wrong. About eight feet of the left outer wing panel was gone. The rudder was gone and the vertical. Other parts, too. One of the engines was feathered. And one of the engines wasn't even on the plane! "So, where's the emergency equipment? How come the alarms aren't going off?" The pilot comes in and makes a normal landing as if nothing had happened, then taxis off onto a revetment somewhere.

As it turned out, he didn't land with his group because his plane had been shot up during a combat mission and, good as the B-24 was, there was no way it could have ever taken off from *his* base. That's because it was Gioia where the bombers were fixed or pronounced dead. The thought sank in – maybe we are at war.

Chapter 7

Bombs Away!

"I could see omens of the war's end almost every day in the blue southern sky when, flying provocatively low, the bombers of the American Fifteenth Air Force crossed the Alps from their Italian bases to attack German industrial targets."

– Albert Speer
Reich Minister of Armaments and War Production

We lived in tents at Torretta, an airfield in Apulia south of Foggia, Italy, located about seven miles from Cerignola and just south of Rome's east line. The Foggia Airfield Complex was made up of about thirty airbases and, because the weather in southern Italy was better than England's, these bases were strategic to bombing missions in Germany, France, Austria, and the Balkans. Our crew had been loaded into the back of an open-ended truck for the thirty-mile trip from Gioia. We jounced along, chilled by the September air of the countryside, and I could feel my excitement growing as I thought about the battles ahead and how we as a crew had been forged into a brotherhood trained to beat the odds.

Upon arrival to Torretta, we received our official combat designation as the 484th Bombardment Group of the 49th Bombardment Wing. We were assigned to the tents that would be home for several months. These were sixteen-foot pyramidal tents with four-foot risers all around and a center pole. Roland, Dick, and Smitty shared quarters with me. There were two bombardment groups, ours and the 461st, and two divided runways. Each group could muster four squadrons at any one time. A squadron was formed by seven planes in a diamond-shaped, three-three-one pattern. When it came time to execute a mission, we were well-oiled machines.

After the sergeant barged into our tents at 4:00 a.m. and rousted us out, we dressed, ate breakfast in the mess hall, and assembled for the briefing where all the details of the mission were covered. An 8 ½-by-14-inch sheet of paper called a flimsy (paper during the war was of poor quality) was given to the command pilots telling us what airplane we'd be flying, where it was located, what position of the formation we'd be in, timings, and so forth.

Instead of communicating via radio, which could have tipped off the Germans that we were coming, the control tower would send differently-colored flares for the commands: "Start engines," "Begin the taxi," and "Take off," signified a double green flare. We'd start the engines, do our runups and checks, and form a line. The first man to take off would taxi out of his revetment. Number two would see him, hit his stopwatch and, at twenty seconds, put on full power. So it went down the line. Then, each squadron leader would take off, make a 180-degree turn, and come to the back side of the runway. Each plane behind him would then turn to get in line to fly on his wing.

The B-24 could hold as much as 8,000 pounds of bombs in its two central bomb bays, either a load of eight 1,000-pound or sixteen 500-pound, depending on the level of damage desired by headquarters. We'd fly to a point pre-positioned for the target, usually fifteen to twenty-five miles from the bomb's strike point. The first plane in the squadron had the bombsight aboard, and the bombardier, once he turned on the device, would strive to get visual contact with the target. Once he did, he would lock it in the bombsight and tell the pilot he had it. The pilot would throw a switch, and the bombsight would guide the plane the rest of the way on the final approach. Everybody had to get super tight in order to make a good bomb pattern on the ground. There was no deviating, even if flak was coming up all over you, because if you deviated, your bombs would be no good and the day would be wasted.

Once the bombs fell out of the first plane, the rest of the bombardiers would hit their switches so the bombs would go down en masse. At least one airplane in every squadron had a camera to document the bomb strike, and these pictures were viewed in the debriefing sessions, along with information given by the crew and noted by a clerk to evaluate the operation.

A disturbing story we heard was about a traitor who had been discovered shortly before our arrival on the base. He was an American who'd sold out to the Germans and was getting paid $1,000 for every B-24 he blew up. The treachery was discovered by a bombardier, who also happened to be the crew armorer and who did not like to attend briefings. It so happened that during one of the missed briefings, he decided to go out to the airplane to check the bombs, guns, and ammunition. During his inspection, he noticed something attached to the nosewheel, a small bomb that had been wired to a switch which showed the nosewheel wasn't bound, so, as soon as the gear started up, the switch would open and voltage across the switch would ignite the bomb. He raced to the building where the briefing was underway and breathlessly reported the explosive. The briefing was canceled, the mission was canceled, and the man was arrested. He admitted that he was sending the money to his family back in the States under the pretense they were his gambling winnings. You see, the Germans knew the B-24 had a design flaw in the fuel transfer system. We'd learned about this in training and also learned techniques to counter the problem. But not all pilots followed the procedure and many planes exploded during take-off. This information gave the Germans a convenient cover to their spy in the camp. Sentenced to death by firing squad, he made a deal with the officers, saying he'd give them all of his Nazi contacts if they would announce that he died in the line of duty. He was shot that very night.

My first mission was on October 4, 1944. We were to bomb a railroad bridge held by the southern boundary, a region of strategic importance to the Allies. The mission was unsuccessful, however, and we had to abort. One of the waist gunner's oxygen tanks was empty, and because we were high flyers and had to go on oxygen at 10,000 feet, we had to turn back with our bomb bays fully loaded.

For my second or third mission – I don't remember exactly – we were assigned another bombing raid in the Po Valley, but this one ended in tragedy. I've never found any record of it, but I know about it because I was there when the tactical officer told us what happened in Po Valley that day.

It was to be a short mission, "a quickie," the briefer said. "What's going to happen is we're going to pound this little town just north of the south rim of the Po Valley. The next day the infantry will come down from the ridge where the front line is and take the town." This was to be part of the Allies' final push of the war in Italy.

The day of the mission was exactly like the day of any bombing mission. Sergeant rouses us at zero dark thirty. We get dressed. Eat breakfast. Go to briefing. Truck picks us up and takes us to the airfield. We get in our planes, move into formation, and take off. We reach the striking point, drop our bombs over a town whose name I don't recall, and return to base. After the raid, we were called in for the debriefing. The tactical officer told us how good we were. He showed us pictures taken by the photo plane that conveyed the density of bomb bursts, our bomb pattern, and other images of the mission.

"The strike was fantastic," he told us. "It really pulverized that town. But there was one little mistake." He hesitated, weighing his words. "You see, somewhere in the hierarchy, the date that the Americans were going to take the town got transmitted incorrectly, and the ground forces went in last night instead of the next. We dropped bombs on 38,000 GIs."

The room sank into stunned silence. I could feel my heart drop to my knees. Someone asked, "How many friendlies were hurt?"

"We don't know," came the answer. "We'll get back to you." But they never did. Nor did we really want to know. To this day I haven't found any record of the catastrophe.

Besides bombing runs in northern Italy, we attacked in Germany, Vienna, Yugoslavia, Bulgaria, and Romania. People often ask me if I was afraid when I went out on a mission. The answer is – no. I didn't have any fear. For one thing, I always figured that if something's going to happen, it's going to happen. But I also had a mental strategy that worked for me like a machine, and that was to concentrate on achieving whatever task was in front of me, one at a time. As I did this, I could write it off as *no problem* and take the next safe step, beginning with the predawn wake-up – *no problem* – breakfast, then the briefing – *no problem* – and all the way to the "Start your engines" colored flare, to launching, to flying the mission, and returning to base. *No problem.* And yet . . .

The clouds were low and heavy the day of the milk run, no more than 200 feet off the ground. You could only see the plane in front of you. Command launched the flight anyway, another bomb run into the Po Valley. We were going to bomb through the overcast on radar. In such conditions, the normal twenty-second intervals were knocked down to ten seconds between take-off power, and you had to get to the guy in front of you as quickly as possible and move into position so you didn't lose sight of him. Being new, I was in the tail end squadron. I got up fast and put the throttles to the wall. The co-pilot put the friction lever on. Below us on the ground were eight Triple A's (anti-aircraft artillery) that had our altitude precisely and were firing steadily. Then it was our turn. We were coming in and passed the I.P. (Initial Point for the bomb run), but before we got to the drop, the first burst came at us.

We rolled off, and I got slightly out of position. When I realized it, I banked into the plane I was supposed to be close to, as close as humanly possible to get the bomb patterned properly on the ground. I'm staring at

41

the pilot beside me when suddenly he gets it in the bomb bay, one of the eights has hit him, and then a blinding yellow-red flash, as if somebody went "click," then – nothing.

There was only one thing for me to do and that was to move up to the next airplane. Of the seven planes that had turned on the IP, there were now only two of us left, due to the black mushrooms of flak coming in all directions. He was in front of me, and I was his wingman on the right. I didn't know if he was deputy lead, or lead, or anything. He broke radio silence (not that it mattered. Hell, the Germans knew we were there anyway) and said, "You better take lead. This is only my sixth mission."

"Well, you're up one on me," I said. "Just go ahead and drop when we think it's right," and that's what we did. His bombardier didn't have a bombsight, nor did I; he just guessed from the previous smokes coming up through the low overcast. We waved off. When the bomb bay released its load, the bombardier said, "Bombs away!" We cut power, dropped, and turned to get out of the guns' range. Problem solved. Time to go home.

To keep from freezing in high altitudes, the B-24 crews wore electrically-heated suits and underwear. As we headed home, I noticed I was getting hot, so I turned back the dial a little on the controller. I was now sweating from the heat, so I turned the dial back some more – several times, in fact. Nothing happened. I hit the stop. No change. "This thing's defective," I thought, and reached down with both hands to a large plug, twisted it, and pulled it out. I put my hand inside to feel the little wires. They were cold. Yet I was broiling. When we got on the ground, I had the suit checked out. Not a thing was wrong with it. Instead, it was my body registering the trauma of those close calls.

The other planes made it back safely, all but one. The only thing left of that plane was pieces of aluminum welded into the side of mine. To think the poor fellow's tent door was only eight feet from mine; we saw each other every day! In fact, I'm still pained by a memory of him shaving right before going on a mission. "Why are you bothering to do that?" I'd asked him. "Who you gonna impress?"

"If *it* ever happens, I want the body to look good."

I walked away, amused, but would soon find only sorrow in recalling the scene. I still play reruns of that mission in my head, images of the B-24 bursting into fiery confetti. My wife, Barbara, recently told me that while recovering from a medical procedure that required anesthesia, I was crying and very agitated about the crew that did not come back.

Low, heavy clouds nearly caused disaster on another assignment. The planes were in position – I was the last one in the formation. I put the throttles to the wall and kept my eyes glued to the plane next to me, maneuvering close on his wing before he got into the clouds. Suddenly, my co-pilot started yelling and pointing at the artificial horizon. Our wings were vertical, with no lift.

"This guy's lost it and I'm under him!" I shouted. The other pilot's wings were generating lift sideways. I looked over and saw that we were only 500 feet from the ground. Now I'm in no man's land. I pushed the nose forward to get out of his way. As soon as I saw him disappear, I leveled off and blind-climbed as fast as I could until I came to the top of the clouds at 13,000 feet or so and finally punched through the white, only to see another plane coming out of the clouds within fifty feet. I wonder how many times we got even closer than that on the way up! There were other incidents when two B-24s came out of the clouds together, but not everyone got out.

Only once on a mission did I see an enemy plane. We were headed to Austria. The temperature that day was extreme – sixty-seven degrees below zero – and on the way to the target, my flight controls froze. To save fuel, we generally would fly in a loose formation until we were close to the target. On the way, there's a designated space where it's safe for the gunners to test-fire their guns, usually over mountains or water. When the gunners attempted to fire, they found the grease so stiff from the cold that even though they could put a shell in the chamber by hand, the next round wouldn't load.

As we approached the target area, I began to tighten up in the formation by dropping my wing briefly toward the lead airplane, then inched closer by rocking the wing a little. But when I tried to raise the wing to stop the approach, I discovered my controls were frozen. I struggled to move the wheel, but it wouldn't budge. Roland got on his wheel and by brute force broke it loose. I turned the autopilot on and the plane was flying well, but I knew I couldn't fly formation that way, so I turned off autopilot and instructed George, the radio operator, to fire the flare to abort.

We headed home and were flying offshore over the Adriatic Sea. Suddenly, I get a call from Glen, the ball turret gunner. "Skipper, I just saw a fighter take off!"

I looked at the altimeter – we were still above 25,000 feet, and I'm thinking, "Boy, the kid must have good eyes." I didn't want to embarrass him, so I said, "Keep an eye on it."

After a while, he called me back and said, "I'm sorry, I lost sight of him."

It so happened that Roland was looking through the side bubble window. On the B-24, the side windows aren't flat, and you could stick your head in that Plexiglass bubble and look straight down or in other directions. All of a sudden, he lurched and banged his head, then turned around and opened his mouth to speak. At the same time, the tail gunner announced, "The bandit's going away. Six o'clock!" The gunner started giving us a play-by-play running of where the fighter was. Meanwhile, George was heading to the back of the plane to use the relief tube when he noticed all the guys were looking out the same side of the airplane.

"What's going on?"

"There's a fighter out there!"

"Well, shoot at him!" George says.

"The gun won't fire," says the waist gunner, Lonnie.

"Why?" asks George.

"Stiff grease," says Lonnie.

Now the radio operator was also trained as a gunner. He pushed Lonnie aside, opened the breach of the gun, and pulled out the block. He wiped it on his flight suit, put it back, and test-fired it. From my seat, I could feel the plane shake. "Somebody's gun is working," I thought. I looked out and damned if it wasn't the Me-109 (Messerschmitt), maneuvering to get behind us! Tracers were going out and falling short. But that was enough for the enemy pilot. He knew he was outgunned. He rolled over and headed straight down. We never saw him again. "George, you saved all of our lives." George had come up to the cockpit and was standing quietly beside me.

"I'm sorry. I was really only test-firing it."

"What are you sorry about?" I said.

"I thought maybe you would be happy to have an airplane painted on the side of our plane" (this was usually done when you had a confirmed kill).

"If you weren't so ugly, I'd kiss you!" I told him.

From October to mid-December 1944, we averaged one mission every four days, with some back to back. The most intense groundfire I encountered was during a mass bombing of Vienna. Intelligence had learned that practically every basement in the city had a lathe, milling machine, or other hardware to be used for German munitions. We were one of 1,500 airplanes of all varieties, and believe me, if you want to feel small, just be one of 1,500 anything at the same time. A well-worn saying among airmen in the war was, "The flak was so thick you could walk across the top of it." That's how it was in Vienna. The flak painted a heavy, black, unending line in the sky. The Germans didn't bother aiming their weapons, which were mounted on flak towers – huge anti-aircraft concrete structures. They knew the altitude we'd be flying, so they simply pointed the guns straight up and fired away nonstop.

For only a few minutes did we get fighter cover from P-51s, but fortunately, none of the B-24s we flew were damaged, except for minor nicks and pings. No one on my plane was ever injured. The only thing that came close was when a shell burst relatively close to the bombardier's window and a chip of Plexiglass hit him in the chin, drawing a drop of blood.

"I'm wounded!" he said with dramatic flair, followed by laughter.

After we returned to the United States in the aftermath of our military service, Dick and I went our own ways but managed to stay in touch. One day he calls and says, "You remember that day the shell burst near my window and I got nicked? I got the Purple Heart for that!"

"No kidding!"

"Yeah, the thing started festering up years later, and I had to go get it lanced. They found a tiny piece of shrapnel in there, and that was enough for me to get the Purple Heart!"

Our adventures in the bomb group had their lighter moments. Dick and I frequently left camp to walk all over the countryside. We never felt threatened. We'd run into farmers and their families, and talk mostly with our hands and many gestures, though Dick spoke a little Italian. Once, walking in a rural area near Cerignola, we heard someone hollering. We looked, and there was a husky farm woman standing at her door, waving for us to come over. Dick and I exchanged glances, then went to the house. She invited us to come in and sit down. No one else was there but us. She took a big, mound-shaped loaf of bread that she'd baked herself, got out a large knife and started sawing away . . . toward herself! I was afraid she'd slip and hurt herself, but apparently, this was her standard method of slicing bread. And oh, man, was that bread delicious. It wasn't dark, but not white either; rather, baked with a natural flour. We ate several pieces before saying *ciao* to this kind and friendly stranger.

On another occasion, a cripple came to live in our tent. On the days we didn't fly, we could do practically anything we wanted. Dick and I would go hunting or target shooting any chance we got. We had quite an arsenal from trading and plenty of ammo, compliments of the U.S. Army, which as I said liked us to practice shooting. Before joining up, Dick's hobby had been taxidermy, so one day he said, "Let's go out in the field, and I'll take my carbine and shoot a magpie. Then I'll bring it home and mount it, and we'll have a pet magpie in the tent."

I'm thinking, "Hmm, a magpie is about the size of a crow and a carbine shoots .30 caliber – wouldn't be much magpie left," but what I said was, "Sure, I'll go along. I'd enjoy the walk."

Once we got to the open country, we spotted a magpie sitting on a high branch about seventy-five yards away, going through his repertoire of songs. The bird belongs to the crow family but sings like a mockingbird and is considered to be one of the most intelligent animals on earth. Dick assumed the standard sitting position with knees and gun, and slowly squeezed the trigger. The bird dropped. My job was to stand there, fixate on where it had fallen, and give Dick signals as to location. The grass was tall – at least a foot high – and I gave Dick right/left to guide him to the spot, then ran over to see what shape the bird was in. He was holding the bird in his hand, and it was looking at us. "What are you going to do with him?" I asked. "Are you going to wring his neck?"

"Well, he's not really hurt that bad," said the intrepid hunter. "Just bleeding a little." The bullet had gone through the joint of a wing, so he had only half a wing on one side. "Do you have any sulphonamide?" This was a kind of wonder drug in powder form used in World War II and known for healing wounds quickly. I kept it in my pocket for any sort of cut. We put a little of it on the bird and sure enough, the bleeding stopped.

"So, Dick, what are you going to do with him?"

"He can't fly anymore. I guess it's up to us to keep him alive. Let's take him back to the tent. He's probably hungry." So, we were going to have a pet in the tent after all!

Back at the tent, we broke into one of the C rations, which included a small tin can of mystery meat and a little wind-up type opener. We opened it up and set it on the tent floor. The magpie wolfed it down immediately. All of a sudden, he realized we were his saviors, so he stayed around, even though the tent door was usually open and he could have left. Poor fellow attempted to fly, but of course it didn't work. He'd get off the ground maybe a foot or so, then flop. He finally accepted it and would walk sideways up the ridge of the tent all the way to the top and sing his heart out. Then one day he figured out that if he sprung up with the good wing and twisted in the air with the good wing down, he could go a little until it got level. Then he'd lose control, fold up, drop down a little, and do it some more. It sure was an ugly looking flight path.

When the OSS called us up, we had to say goodbye to our funny magpie. To think we never even gave him a name.

Chapter 8

Code Name "Arise"

"They did whatever was necessary, using trickery, subterfuge, exotic weapons, and nerves of steel to slip in among the enemy and accomplish things that might be impossible for an entire battalion of soldiers to do."
– Gregory A. Freeman
The Forgotten 500

Our fourteenth and final bombing mission was on November 21, 1944. A couple of days later, the group commander said, "Okay, pack up. Here's your orders." Six of us from the crew were assigned to the 885th Heavy Special Bombardment Squadron of the Fifteenth Air Force in Brandisi, Italy. Before being transferred, I asked the commander what I'd be doing when I got there. All he said was, "You'll find out."

It was only much later that we learned the 885th was a front for the OSS – Office of Strategic Services, the forerunner of the Central Intelligence Agency. What we did know was that we wouldn't be releasing bombs but supplies and agents dropped at low altitudes behind enemy lines. With people, we dropped to 600 feet. With materiel (military equipment and supplies), 300 feet. We didn't rely on paper-documented altitude elevations. We relied on the radar altimeter on board to show us accurately how high we were off the ground. The device was very advanced for its time and is still used on some airplanes today.

Besides myself, there were my co-pilot, Roland; the navigator, Smitty; the bombardier, Dick; the flight engineer, Warren; and the radio operator, George. We rode in the back of a truck and arrived at the airfield in Brindisi (code name "Arise") four hours later. Brindisi, located on the Adriatic coast of Italy almost to the heel, was about sixty-six miles south of the OSS headquarters in Bari, also on the coast. After settling into our new billets, we were assigned a side gunner named Daniel Halperin and a tail gunner, Jim O'Flarity. We were then briefed on the nature of our missions –

to make strategic drops beyond the front to support resistance and Allied espionage efforts. Every mission had a code name, like "Slipway Yellow," "Watermelon," and "Pappy."

To improve the success of our trips, we flew at night in the valleys of the Alps, with targets in Austria, North Italy, Yugoslavia, and Romania. We went on 100 percent oxygen at the start of each mission, even though we were flying low. This was because the oxygen improved our vision. We could see where we were going, and our navigation was excellent. Once, flying along in pitch-black darkness, we saw someone on the ground light a cigarette, and suddenly the entire compound below was illuminated by a single match.

We dropped parachute containers with food, leaflets, medical supplies, explosives, gold coins, and small arms. We dropped non-parachute items like clothing, tenting, and bedding that was bundled up and tossed out of the plane. And we dropped OSS agents.

The B-24 Liberator was modified for these clandestine operations. The olive drab was painted gloss black, then polished. Our crew even held Simoniz (wax) parties every month to polish the big bird. Because we were flying at night, we needed to be invisible to enemy searchlights, and the black paint did a good job of it, unlike the irregular texture of the flat olive drab that caught every point of light in every part of the plane. Another alteration was removal of the ball turret, making a well where the agents sat – in our case, no more than three per mission – until they were tapped to go. The space was walled in with smooth metal to avoid any snags.

After arriving in Brindisi, we had only two days of training. On the first day, November 27, we were sent on a practice run with a bombardier from another crew who was considered the expert, with more missions logged than us. He gave us pointers on how to get parachutes and free drops to their intended destinations. Standing behind Dick, who was riding in the front turret, the bombardier in charge gave instructions over the intercom, saying, "The first time, we'll just do a low pass."

He gave me right and left cues to position the airplane where he wanted it and set the distance for parachutes at 300 feet. "A little lower, a little lower," he said, relying on visual recognition instead of an altimeter reading. When he said, "Okay, this is a good place. Let's go around and do a dry run," I made a big racetrack pattern to lose altitude and went back to reposition.

Dick, who would be giving the drop command during an actual mission, nodded his head and said, "Now!"

The timing and positioning satisfied our expert trainer. "Very good," he said. "Let's do it for real this time." By "real," he didn't mean we'd be dropping anyone or anything, but just simulating an actual mission.

Dick gave the okay for the trainer to open the bomb doors. On an authentic mission, Dick would have done the job, but because he was inside the front turret, he didn't have access to the bombardier's controls. "Make a racetrack pattern," Dick said, so I peeled off to the left, bringing us out over the Brindisi harbor. This was a highly active seaport where materiel was coming in for the British. We had descended to about 250 feet over the water when suddenly I heard a loud "wham!" and looked back to see the bomb doors flapping. The load was gone – the small arms munitions intended for the underground on our next mission, which was to be that very night! The "experienced" bombardier had accidentally yanked the emergency salvo lever, releasing the explosives that landed on a British warship! Fortunately, no one was injured, but it created an international incident and drew a profuse apology from the bombardier, who should have known his right from his left. Needless to say, we didn't fly that night.

Two days later we had another practice drop. This one went smoothly. That was the extent of our training, the sum of our preparation for the dangerous and critical missions ahead. OSS agents were called "Joes," except for a "Josephine" who flew with us once, and we never saw their faces. These measures to conceal their identities were taken in case we were captured by the Germans and ordered to reveal their names. During the approach to the drop zone, the dispatcher, Jim O'Flarity, who was also my tail gunner, would stand behind the agents sitting around the "Joe Hole," as it was called, and discuss the order they'd be going in. On the bombardier's signal, Jim removed the plywood covering the hole and tapped the agents to exit as quickly as possible so they'd get ahead of the supply parachutes we would be dropping in the next pass to avoid any entanglement.

We flew away, then returned, watching for the signal that told us the "Joes" had made it down safely. Then we released the supply parachutes. Once, we ran into trouble with an Italian agent. He was the sole agent on that flight and didn't speak English. As we approached the drop zone on the Swiss side of Italy, he panicked, turned around, and grabbed O'Flarity. The two men grappled for a couple of minutes, but O'Flarity managed to subdue him, and out he went.

The OSS shared the Brindisi air base with its British counterpart, the SOE: Special Operations Executive. The American planes were the B-24, the B-17, the P-38, and the C-47. The British planes were the Lancaster, the

Seafire, which was the marine version of the Spitfire, and the Wellington, which was almost completely made of wood. These aircraft all did different jobs. For example, once the OSS discovered that the Germans were supplying the Italians' light barges at night, they would use radar to spot them; then the Wellingtons would go and sink the barges.

The C-47 missions were especially treacherous, and I admired the men who flew them. They did the same work we did, dropping people and supplies behind enemy lines, only they landed on primitive runways in the dark to pick up downed aviators – a great many from Yugoslavia and Bulgaria – that the underground had rescued. Then they'd take off. The guesswork in those night-time conditions was unimaginable. The landing area was defined by two people – members of the resistance – who aimed flashlights in the direction the plane would be coming from. One flashlight was covered with green cellophane and one with red. To concentrate the light, they taped the tube of a paper towel on each lens.

The airmen had no way of knowing the runway length. I talked to some of those pilots, and they told me, "You had to slow the damn thing down as much as possible and aim for the green light." As soon as they passed the green, they put the plane on the ground no matter what the ground was. The guys with flashlights had been trained to flatten themselves on the ground as the airplane flew over them, and the pilots were trained to get the wheels on the ground as soon as they passed the green light. Never, ever were the pilots to go beyond the red signal light because there might not be any more anything! As if by magic, partisans would come out of the woods and empty the plane of supplies – quick, quick, quick! As soon as it was emptied, another group would emerge, bringing with them aviators from various bomb groups that had been shot down, Americans and English they'd hidden from the Nazis and risked their lives in doing so. They'd herd the airmen into the C-47, which would take off for the Foggia airfield. A book about the rescue of 500 American downed aviators from Yugoslavia is told in thrilling detail by Gregory A. Freeman in *The Forgotten 500*.

Some of our drops were containers made of cheap, thin metal and filled with international gold coins with a total weight, including the parachute, of 500 pounds. The coins were used at the discretion of partisans and agents for bribing Germans. For example, a Nazi might be judged to be on the edge of loyalties, or a town officer might be bribed to work for the Allies. Of course, there was also the risk that the gold would fall into Nazi hands. So, we always turned off the salvo switch when parachuting the gold.

One night, four officers from a crew billeted a couple of doors down from us came in all liquored up and began bragging that they'd kept one of the containers. "We dropped it in the Alps, but no one but us will ever be able to find it," said one of the men. "After the war, we'll get that gold alright, won't we, boys?"

I couldn't help wondering if that was the drunk talking or if they really had hidden the gold, which back then was worth around thirty-five dollars an ounce. (Today it's worth about 1,300 dollars an ounce.) The only thing I did learn was the news that several days later, on a daylight mission, those boys flew into the side of a mountain. Tragically, all eight crew members died. I'm familiar with the details of the mission because it's one I had previously been sent on, and I learned from pre-flight that I'd have to adjust for the fact that the floor of that valley climbed faster than a B-24 could climb. So, when I got to the top of the valley, I deliberately stalled the plane and let it fall into the cut, dropped the materiel, then calmly circled up. The pilot who crashed into the mountain was attempting to climb out and couldn't clear the ridge, so he decided to turn and didn't make it. I have a photograph of one of the engines that rolled down the hill in the snow. It's a surreal reminder of the lightning-swift changes in fortune that war always brings.

As mentioned, there was always the danger of our supply drops being captured by the enemy. This was the case with an entire field hospital that was dropped in Yugoslavia. I didn't fly that mission, but we heard about the atrocities inflicted by the Ustaše when they came upon the hospital, confiscated it, and tortured the doctor and nurses. The Ustaše was a faction of the Croatian Revolutionary Movement that mixed fascism, Roman Catholicism, and ultra-nationalism. They bound the doctor to a table, spread out his hands, and put scalpels in each of his fingers right through to the wood. Nurses were also found, their breasts stabbed into the table. That's how the partisans discovered some of the victims still alive. They died slow, excruciating deaths. It was well known that these Ustaše were worse than Nazis. Some said they made the Germans look like Boy Scouts! I even heard an account of a skirmish between Nazis and partisans. The Ustaše came on the scene and wanted to steal the goods we'd given them. The Nazis and the partisans joined forces and drove off the members of the Ustaše they hadn't killed. When it was all over, the Nazis and partisans shook hands and departed.

I've always been enormously grateful for being spared most of the war's horrors. I attribute this in part to my good fortune of being an airman instead of an infantryman. After the Japanese bombed Pearl Harbor but before I actually enlisted, I ran into a guy on leave who was the big brother of a high school classmate. This was in '42. He'd enlisted in the infantry well before Pearl and was stationed in a facility in the middle of the island of Oahu. All he got was a kind of side view of the bombing, but what he saw of the burning wreckage of American ships made him fiercely bitter.

This is what he said: "The best thing I can do is ram a bayonet through the belly of a pregnant Jap. Then I get two, for one stab." I knew damn well I didn't want to be in that kind of an army. A lot of people felt that way. I was lucky in so many, many ways during that terrible war. I didn't even know about the genocide of the Jews until after the war. The media shielded the public from such grim realities. I'll always be thankful that I and my crew kept aloft in the B-24s I flew and were never shot down but lived to tell our tales. The most harrowing and momentous of these was called Operation Greenup.

Chapter 9

Operation Greenup

Until I came to the end credits, I sat through the whole movie without realizing it was inspired by Operation Greenup and OSS agent Fred Mayer. The vengeful Jewish-American soldiers in the fictionalized *Inglourious Basterds* resembled Mayer only in the respect that he was a German-born Jew who sought revenge against the Nazis. For Fred and his fellow agents, also European-born Jews, victory was achieved not by scalping German heads but by infiltrating enemy ranks to gain vital intelligence. Greenup was one of the most successful covert missions of World War II, saving thousands of lives and accelerating the war's end in Europe. If you want to know the real story about Fred and Operation Greenup, watch *The Real Inglorious Bastards*, a documentary made in 2012. Fred was my hero and closest friend until his death on April 15, 2016, at age ninety-four.

The war in Europe was finally grinding down, and by the winter of 1945, the Germans were on the run. Innsbruck, their last stronghold, was the most heavily fortified territory of the Third Reich. The OSS needed to gather intelligence regarding Nazi movements of munitions and supplies down through the Brenner Pass, which forms the border between Italy and Austria. This was a mystery because all the railroad bridges going through the pass had been bombed by Allied planes, yet supplies were still getting through.

The top-secret mission was to drop three agents behind enemy lines over a frozen lake 10,000 feet above sea level in the Austrian Alps. The steep mountain peaks were heavily guarded by anti-aircraft, and the operation was so dangerous that the British Royal Air Force, as I learned later, refused to go. Naturally, I signed up for the job. "If they're crazy enough to jump there," I told the officer, "I'll be crazy enough to take them."

On a cold, dark night – the date was February 20, 1945 – a windowless panel truck from headquarters in Bari pulled up under the wing of my B-24. As always, I'd started the engines at the designated time, checked them

53

out, then taxied to the end of the runway where our crew was waiting for the "Joes'" arrival. From the cockpit, we couldn't see the three agents and dispatcher/jumpmaster as they climbed out of the truck and headed to the rear of the plane. The truck backed out, and an officer walked around to signal me that all was clear. I could feel the adrenaline pumping as I took off, excited to be on such an important mission. Two hours later, as we were en route to the target point, I got this message from a radio operator: "In the event there is no reception," she said, "or if you can't see the drop site, or if for any reason you can't complete the mission, *do not* return to home base, but instead, go to Cyphon." That was the code name for Rosignano Airfield, about 500 miles from Brindisi.

We climbed until we were over the Alps and at the drop site. Smitty, the navigator, said he knew the lake was below us. Imagine a giant soup bowl with a rim about 13,000 feet above sea level, whereas the drop zone was 10,000 feet. We were supposed to drop the agents into the bowl. The only problem was, we couldn't *see* anything because of heavy cloud cover. There was no way I was going to let three men jump out of the plane without being able to see the ground, even though I had every confidence in Smitty for accuracy. It was too much to ask. We flew off for about twenty miles and stayed on a straight line, then turned around on the same line to take another look. It was still a no-go. So, we went to the alternate Rosignano. Our passengers remained incognito as they were directed to their tents for the night and we to ours.

In line at the mess hall for breakfast the next morning, I spotted the four strangers, all of whom appeared to be in their early twenties, and introduced myself and my crew. "Won't you join us at our table?" I asked, gesturing for them to sit down. Now, the only thing we knew about these men is that we were taking them on a secret mission to gain intelligence. As their identities were concealed, the information I include following each agent's name is what I learned much later.

The team leader was a good-looking, dark-haired man of slight build. "Joe," AKA Fred Mayer, was the son of Jewish parents and born in the Black Forest area of Germany. His father, Heinrich, had been awarded an Iron Cross in the German Army in World War I. When the Nazis came to power, his wife begged him to leave, but he said, "No, they're not going to bother me. I'm a war hero! My distinguished military record will protect us." But with growing antisemitism, the handwriting was on the wall for Jews. Heinrich realized he had to get his family out of the country and moved them to Brooklyn in 1938.

After high school, Fred worked as a diesel mechanic, and when Pearl Harbor was bombed, he joined the army. To show you the stuff he was made of, when he was in training and playing war games, he went to the mock headquarters and arrested the brigadier general running the exercise. The general protested that he was breaking the rules, but Fred stood his ground. "The rules of war are to win," he said. Afterwards, at the briefing to discuss the success of the "war," the general told him he was in the wrong outfit. "You need to be in intelligence."

Fred was indeed the ideal OSS candidate and absolutely fearless. He was a risk-taker, spoke German and two other European languages, and was trained in demolition, hand-to-hand combat, and other martial skills. Officials at the OSS headquarters in Bari wanted to give him a forged document that would allow him to get away with things when he was doing his spy stuff. "No," he said. "I don't want it. You can give it to me, but I'll just throw it away. I'll handle things myself." As we sat around the table drinking coffee, Dick started speaking to Fred in German. He, too, had German parents and the two men seemed to have quite a lot to talk about.

The second "Joe" was the radio operator, a Dutch boy named Hans Wynbert. He had a long face, a big grin, and indeed looked like a schoolboy. Like Fred, he was also Jewish. Hans and his twin brother had been sent to America by their parents to escape the Nazis in Holland. Tragically, his mother, father, and younger brother were captured, sent to Auschwitz, and never heard from again.

The third agent was Franz Weber. He was Austrian, a devout Catholic, and a disaffected officer in the Wehrmacht. He had intentionally gotten too close to the front lines so he could be captured. With the OSS needing more European recruits to infiltrate the enemy, Fred dressed as a German officer and slipped into a POW camp in southern Italy, pretending to be a prisoner. There he found Franz and persuaded him to become the third member of the Operation Greenup team. Of great advantage was the fact that Weber's family lived near Innsbruck in a village called Oberperfuss that would later become a protective home base for the agents.

The fourth "Joe" was Walter Hass, the jumpmaster, also Jewish. He'd fled Nazi Germany with his family and eventually emigrated to America. Recruited by the OSS, his job was to check the equipment and oversee the parachute jumps to ensure safety and timing. Normally, as mentioned, personnel would be dropped at 600 feet altitude and supplies at 300. Fred demanded we drop the agents at 300 to avoid radar detection. "My best wish would be for the parachute to open and my feet touch the ground," he said. That was a little too much precision to ask for!

The next day, a P-38 Lockheed Lightning was sent out to check on the weather to see if conditions were suitable for our mission. Now, the P-38 was a great fighter plane but also excellent for recon missions and equipped with the most sophisticated cameras of their time. To lighten the plane so it could fly high and fast, there were no guns aboard. When the pilot came back, he said, "Don't even try." So, we spent the entire day together sitting around and swapping stories.

The third day, another no-go, was the day I let Fred fly my plane. Fred could tell you anything, and in fact, he *did* tell me anything, including his aviation background, all the airplanes he'd flown – he even told me about the time he stole a Junkers airplane from Franco. The way he talked, you couldn't *not* believe. So, when we found out that we weren't going down that day, Smitty asked if we could go on a short test flight to check out the accuracy of the airspeed gauges. He always wanted to calibrate everything to the nth degree, so I agreed. Then I told Fred we'd be going on a test ride.

"You want to come along and fly the airplane?" I asked.

"Ja," he said, and before long, he was in the co-pilot's seat. He admitted he'd flown many airplanes except for the B-24 and said for me to do take-off and landing – he could handle everything else.

We took off from Rosignano and did our calibration run. Afterward, I said, "Okay, Fred, it's your airplane." Without a blink, he pulled the power back and leveled off over the harbor at about a hundred feet, the height of a sailboat mast. Then he flew toward a cut in the mountain on the shore and did a beautiful Immelmann. (This is a half loop followed by a half roll. It reverses direction and increases altitude.) I thought, "Boy, is he a good aviator!" The whole flight lasted about thirty-five minutes.

Several weeks later, Colonel Monroe McClusky summoned me to his office at Brindisi. For what seemed an eternity, I stood at attention in front of his desk. Finally, he spoke. "So, why did you buzz the base headquarters at Rosignano? What in the hell am I supposed to tell the base commander?"

"Well, sir, I didn't really have a reason. But honest, I didn't know it was headquarters."

"NOW you know where it is, and as a matter of fact, we're going to be moving there soon!" I didn't say a word about Fred who, by then, was undercover in enemy territory. Many years afterward, Fred admitted that he'd had exactly one glider lesson! He was a natural-born pilot. I've never known anyone like him. In fact, I was quoted in a *New York Times* story that came out after his death. "I was in awe of him. He was born without the fear gene. He feared nothing, and he was able to be whatever he needed to be."

On February 23, the P-38 came back and reported large breaks in the clouds over the Alps. Again, we launched. Six hours and fifteen minutes later, we arrived at the designated site, only to see heavy overcast and no visibility. On the 24th, we stood down again, but that night, Fred, Walter, Smitty, and Dick pored over the maps and found a secondary site. "This will work," Smitty said. "It's a bit farther away and will delay the arrival in Innsbruck by a day. But it would save the mission."

The next day, February 25, we were given the okay to go, and this time we were determined to make it happen. Franz was wearing a German officer's uniform. Fred and Hans had on flight suits posing as American aviators. The idea was that right after touchdown, if some junior German officer might come upon them, Franz was going to say, "These are my prisoners. I'm taking credit for them. Get lost!"

On arriving at the location about three hours later, there was nothing but white, absolute white. We flew off and came back a couple of times with hopes the clouds had cleared, but not even a pinnacle was in sight. So, we went to the alternate drop zone. This was over a valley and even lower than the original site. I cleared the rim, then took the power off all four engines and started down. Instantly I realized, "We are going down too fast!" Too late, I remembered what we'd been told before departure – that the wind speed at the top of the Alps that night was going to be over 200 miles per hour! When the wind crested the rim and began racing down from its lateral direction, it became what's called a foehn wind. For every foot that it descends, the air itself gets heavier and therefore accelerates.

I realized the problem right away and put the throttles to full power, which meant that each of the four engines was putting out 1,000 horsepower. It wasn't enough. I put it up to take-off power – 1,200 horsepower per engine – but we continued our deadly plunge. It's a strange thing, but even with my B-24 being drawn down by that horrific wind, time went into slow motion, and I felt completely calm. "Okay," I thought. "Time for emergency power." At a setting of 1,450 horsepower per engine, it was to be used only in a war emergency and for no longer than five minutes. That's actually 250 horsepower more than the maximum take-off power Pratt and Whitney, the designer, said the engine could withstand. But it still wasn't enough. We kept dropping down and down. So I released the latch on the turbo control and went to a full stop. This gave us the maximum 25,000 rpm of the turbines in the turbo supercharger. It resulted in an increase in the manifold pressure; this had gone completely off scale. We had no idea how greatly we were straining the engines, but adding power enabled us to slow our descent. We were also fortunate that the freezing weather kept the engines from overheating. Suddenly, to our enormous relief, the plane stopped falling, most likely because the air mass had no place to go but level. The wind simply couldn't blow down anymore. Now, it was time to get out of there.

The easiest route would have been to turn southward and fly down the valley into the Brenner Pass, eventually descending to sea level and the Adriatic Sea. That, of course, was not an option, considering that the pass was the densest anti-aircraft section of all Nazi Germany and its captured grounds. Instead, I flew back and forth, back and forth across the valley, gaining altitude as I went. At first, the zigzags were only a matter of seconds because the valley was so narrow, but little by little we made our ascent. I may have been misled but I was confident in the ability of the airplane, especially in the low levels of the valley. I flew as close as I could to the mountain wall, then reversed. Dick in the front seat would say, "Turn, John."

When I asked him later, during debriefing, "How close did I get to the mountain wall?" he said he could count how many pine needles were on the trees!

Finally, twenty-two minutes later, we reached the mountain peak at an altitude of over 13,000 feet. Smitty recorded every minute detail of that trip and said that from the time I closed the throttles to the time we reached the base of the valley was *eighteen seconds and a drop of 6,000 feet!* Later, Roland, who as co-pilot had handled all the cooling and power settings, told me that not one instrument had gone out of the green, due to temperatures somewhere between fifty and sixty degrees below zero. Once we returned to normal power, we double-checked everything and decided we'd better go home.

"But first," I said, "let's go back over the primary target." We flew back to the site, and lo and behold, it was wide open! We made a run for it and the agents, one after another, parachuted down.

Now Fred had never used a parachute and neither had the others, but in true Mayer fashion, he told them, "There's nothing to it! You'll love it!" He had a leg bag strapped between both legs that must have weighed a little more than he did. It held money and supplies. When he jumped out, the first thing he did was pull the release, allowing the bag to drop fast for about thirty feet of rope. This lightened his weight and slowed him down before he hit the ground. We went out on our straight line again, then returned to the drop site. Fred flashed us the green "all is well" signal. We dropped the rest of the containers by parachute from the bomb bay. Each weighed 500 pounds and contained food for three days, first aid supplies, and other essentials. We also shoved three soft bags of unbreakable items through the "Joe Hole," including skis. Then we turned around, relieved to have completed our critical mission, and went on a westward course to Brindisi, flying through valleys to avoid radar detection. We stopped at Rosignano for fuel and arrived on base the morning of February 26. All totaled, the mission took over nineteen hours, three flying days, and five full days away from our base.

It wasn't until April 1945 that we learned what had happened to the agents after they jumped and that the operation had been a success. They landed in snow nearly waist high, which fortunately softened the impact of landing. One of the free-falling bags containing a pair of skis missed the target and most likely sailed over the precipice. The men decided to take the other skis and make a toboggan, using the four ski poles as brakes. Years afterward, Fred told me that the sled went so fast that the tip of his ski pole glowed red from his using it to slow down. He said it was the scariest ride of his life.

The first night, they got as far as 7,000 feet elevation from the drop zone of 10,000 feet and slept in a mountain shack equipped with emergency provisions for skiers, compliments of the Austrian government. The next day, they waited until dark to travel to Oberperfuss, where Franz's family and his girlfriend lived. Franz directed the agents to safe havens, Fred to the attic of the Crown Hotel and Hans to a private residence. The house where Hans was hidden resembled many other such houses in the town, perched on a mountainside and having no level places. The front door was on the south side of the house. If you went straight ahead, you'd be in the basement, so you had to take steps to enter the front door. There were three floors above the basement and on each floor, window boxes with potted plants and flowers. Clothes lines also were strung from the windows. One of these was Hans' antennae.

On his first night in Innsbruck, and after curfew, Fred walked brazenly down the middle of the street wearing Weber's German officer's uniform and with his head wrapped in a bandage. He was looking for a Nazi GI. Spotting a soldier way up ahead, he yelled at the top of his lungs, "I've been robbed!" then ran toward the German. "I have nothing!" he cried, turning his pockets inside out to show he had no money. "They took everything – they took all my papers!"

The soldier, a big man about six feet tall, clapped his arm around Fred, five-foot-five Jew that he was, and said, "Calm down. Come with me and I'll help you." He took him to the Innsbruck headquarters where he photographed and fingerprinted him. Fred didn't need a false ID. He had the real thing!

As I mentioned, the intelligence gathered by these incredibly brave men and the network of underground informants they organized turned the tide of war. Of particular significance was stunning information Fred acquired that solved the mystery of how enemy supplies could possibly be moving through the Brenner Pass since the bridges had been bombed, leaving massive wreckage at the bottom of the valley. Fred had learned that every night the trains would leave Innsbruck for Italy. Now Germans in general are very smart. They engineered a way to build a cable suspension bridge that they hid in the mountain tunnels during the day and extended at night from each end of the valley where the trains could cross after dark. The cable ends were attached to cliffs above the track and were somehow concealed during the daytime to avoid being detected. Some of the bridges were nearly half a mile long! Once the Allies found out about the transports, the night flyers went in and did them in. According to an article in the *Army Times,* as reported on West Virginia Senator Jay Rockefeller's former website, the intelligence gathered by Fred "allowed the U.S. Army Air Forces to bomb twenty-six Nazi military trains, [thus] blocking the Brenner Pass."

Chapter 10

Rosignano

My longest mission and one I'm especially proud of occurred the night the Russians took back Vienna. We could actually see the attack happening. We were to serve an underground group outside of Prague and flew to our drop site, where we delivered the containers (one had the gold). When we went by Vienna we could see there was no chance of escape for the Nazis. A round would be fired – *boom!* Then the *blub-blub-blub* that let us know they were goners. It was a long mission, though not a particularly rough one, and when we completed it, we went home. Two other crews were supposed to have gone as well, and upon our return, instead of debriefing us as a crew, the officials sent us to rooms individually and questioned us.

"What about that line of thunderstorms over the Alps?" they asked me.

"We didn't have any. There weren't any high winds at all." None of my crew had the slightest idea of what was going on.

For the next couple of missions, a senior officer accompanied us on our trips, strictly as an observer. Long afterwards, we found out that one of the other airplanes assigned to the Vienna mission was seen over the Mediterranean circling for hours at low altitude. From the moonlight, the British navy figured out it was a B-24 and wanted to know what that pilot was doing out there. The plane had salvo'd its load somewhere over the mountains because, according to that crew, they were in such a violent thunderstorm they couldn't control the airplane. When they returned, the bomb doors were all ruined from the salvo, as they'd dropped the load right through the bomb bay. That put big question marks on us for saying we'd had no trouble getting to the drop site. Fortunately, about three weeks later, the ground recipients in Prague reported that they were very happy for getting at least one airplane-load of materiel. At the very least, those two other crews were cowards! But no disciplinary action was ever taken, and nobody said a word. Back then there were no lengthy judicial hearings or anything of the kind.

As before, we lived in tents with four officers in each. The non-commissioned were tented in another area. A big central tent had showers and other facilities. To the west of the billet was the edge of a cliff overlooking the Mediterranean Sea. To the east was a road and railroad tracks leading to Rome. Nearby was a Chianti winery and beside it, a cheese factory that produced Parmesan. The scents wafting from these two places were to me, a young soldier with unacquired taste, nauseating. Once, we were walking to headquarters and stopped by the winery. People who worked there invited us in and gave us samples. I thought it was the worst stuff in the world! Today I love both Parmesan and Chianti. Now that is growth and maturity.

My tentmates and I chipped in to hire a laundry woman who lived in town. She didn't speak English, but Dick, who was good at languages, was able to translate from Italian. Before that, we had to take our clothes to the base laundry. It was nice having someone else to do the wash. Jim O'Flarity and three other non-com back crew members decided to rent rooms from private citizens instead of living in tents. One day Jim invited me and our whole crew to come downtown to his place for dinner. It was within walking distance and in an area that had been bombed. All the buildings were damaged; rubble was everywhere. Dick and I arrived first. When we got to the door, we looked at each other doubtfully, unsure if it was safe to step inside. The house was dilapidated, with big holes and broken windows. There hadn't been time yet for anyone to rebuild.

We knocked, and a woman of ample stature who looked to be in her thirties, answered. "Come in," she said with a big smile. The doors were solid mahogany and, while the house looked dreadful from outside, the interior, though looking worn, was quite beautiful. Soon, the others arrived, and we sat down at the table.

Our hostess commanded a good bit of English and served a tasty, traditional Italian dinner. Near the end of the meal, Jim gave each of us officers two panels of nylon parachute. He admitted that he and the others on the back crew – Warren Eldridge, George Boyas, and Daniel Halperin – had stolen them off containers meant for the partisans. "I feel very bad about what I did," he said. "I promise I'll never do anything like that again. But since it's already done, you all can use the parachute pieces to bargain with the local people for goods." While he vowed never to do it again and was humble and contrite, he was, nevertheless, the ringleader and it was my duty to report the men.

But mentally, I couldn't go there. I held eye contact with all the crewmen and a brief, wordless conversation with the other officers, Dick, Smitty, and

Roland, whom I could almost hear in my head agreeing with me and the decision they somehow knew I was making. No, I would not turn Jim and the others in, even though I knew the decision made me complicit. I needed that crew; they were the non-com officers and essential to our missions. So, while I could feel guilt gnawing at me, I couldn't report the infraction. Smitty took his two panels home. I don't know what Roland did with his. Dick and I gave ours to the laundry lady, who gave us big hugs in return. Later she invited us for dinner. We accepted, of course.

When the time came, we walked to her house and went to the back door, as we'd been asked to do. This was on the ground floor of a spacious Italian villa situated on a cliff overlooking the Mediterranean. We knocked at the door, thinking these had been or still were the servants' quarters. Our laundry lady answered and invited us in. She introduced us to her husband and two pretty, dark-haired daughters. I'm guessing the oldest was around fifteen and the younger, maybe seven or eight.

The lady had been ironing, but she turned with a smile and said something lyrical in Italian, which translated: "Man's work is sun to sun . . ." Then she spoke to the younger daughter, who vanished into another room. Minutes passed. When she returned, we oohed and aahed in admiration, for she was adorned in a beautiful white dress. She happily danced and modeled it for us, and her mother said, "It's for her confirmation. Made from your parachute!" This made me feel better about the theft and my cover up. The little girl continued to dance around the room, reciting something like, *"Uncie, doonsie . . ."* Dick looked at me and said, "One, two, buckle my shoe."

Then it was time to sit down for a splendid dinner of eggplant Parmesan. After we ate, the husband started talking excitedly, but all I could get was *"boomba!"* Dick turned to me and said, "I think he means there's a bomb upstairs." We asked him to show us. He took us to the front door, and we looked up to see a hole in the ceiling and roof – a hole that was very much over our heads at the table where we had just eaten – and there jutting through the hole was a 500-pound U.S. bomb that had failed to go off. It wasn't damaged at all and even had a serial number! Sometimes years later those things would voluntarily blow up.

The next day I wasted no time in reporting what I'd seen to Colonel McClusky. The house was soon swarming with all kinds of personnel and equipment. Apparently, the bomb had been dropped less than eight months prior to that time. Rosignano had formerly been a Nazi airport that the Allies pretty much destroyed to stop the movement of enemy planes sent over Allied troops trying to invade Italy. Afterward, engineers were sent in to build a new runway and complete other repairs. The bomb in the villa was deactivated in no time and removed. From that day until we left Italy for home, the laundry lady wouldn't accept a single lira for doing our wash.

My last mission, code-named "Slippery Yellow," was on March 18, 1945, and flown out of Rosignano, where we'd been reassigned to be closer to the front lines south of Pisa. We were to drop materiel in the Po Valley, but since we received no reception, the mission was incomplete. That would have been my fortieth OSS mission. For both the bomb group and the OSS, we were given points for executed missions. When you reached fifty, you could go home.

Sometimes a mission would be rough enough that you'd get two points for it. In the bomb group, you had to deliver the bombs to get at least one point. Once, we were going to drop bombs on troops in Yugoslavia after a Nazi column was discovered going south into that country. We were dispatched with anti-personnel bombs, thousands of six-pound bombs with a three-foot stick that hit the ground first, followed by the six pounders, which were like hand grenades, only heavier, and they would go off.

The idea was that these bombs would send the shrapnel sideways, disabling the troops through injury rather than mass killing everybody and thus slow down the attack or even eliminate it altogether. But the weather was so bad we couldn't find the column and had to turn around. I also got points for our attempts to drop Fred and the other OSS agents onto the glacial lake in the Alps; three points, in fact, even though only one mission was actually completed. The powers that be decided that the effort along with the dangerous conditions deserved credit. By the time I left the OSS, I had acquired fifty points – fourteen with the bomb group and thirty-nine with the OSS – enough to go home.

Chapter 11

Post-War Transitions

May 8, 1945, was momentous. It was the day I left Naples for America on a converted "luxury" cruise ship called the USS *West Point*. It was designed to hold 1,200 passengers, only there were 12,000 aboard, plus my crew! The day was momentous for another reason. It was VE or Victory in Europe Day. Three hours after we embarked, the captain's voice trumpeted over the loudspeaker, "Germany has surrendered unconditionally! The war in Europe is over!" Emotions ran high on the ship, with cheering and shouting. For six long days we sailed, and I held up pretty well until right after we passed through the Strait of Gibraltar. I was more bent than straight at that point; it was my first encounter with seasickness.

The sixth day brought us close to Staten Island, but there was still no sight of land. We were all ordered to the bunk site and told to pack and stand by. The place was entirely without windows. Even so, I could feel excitement growing as I assembled my gear and thought of how I would soon be standing safely on American ground. On arrival, we lined up and passed through the ship's massive doors at dock level, then climbed directly into the waiting trucks with their canvas covers. From there we rode to the mess hall in Fort Dix, New Jersey, where we were served a big and most welcome bowl of ice cream, followed by a juicy steak. Now we knew we were home! Best of all, we were given a thirty-day leave.

After a couple of days back in Scituate with my family, I went to Cranston, Rhode Island, a suburb of Providence, to marry my childhood sweetheart. I was almost present at Nancy Gardiner's birth. She was born in 1926, and as a three-year-old, I first knew her as a squalling little thing. My mother and her mother, Edna Mitten Gardiner, had been classmates in Winchester, Massachusetts. Her father's name was Nelson E. Gardiner. He was a master mariner on Liberty ships during the war. Liberty ships were made at the Fore River Shipyard in Quincy, Massachusetts, and Quincy is where I had my first flying lesson. Her family came often to

Scituate for a visit, and our family would visit hers as well. Nancy and I started dating as teenagers. She was pretty, dark-haired, and petite. I often took her dancing in Rhode Island and once, to Boston for a dinner dance in a ballroom where Guy Lombardo was playing "the most danceable music on earth!" What fun we had in that period leading up to the war when Swing was king. Every large city had a ballroom.

We were married in the Gardiner's family church in Cranston. Nancy was a beautiful bride and simply glowed in her white wedding dress. The biggest disappointment was my parents' absence. Even though they were lifelong friends of the Gardiners, they disapproved in general of the marriage, thinking I was too young at twenty-one. Nancy was only eighteen, but we had made the decision to marry after the war and that was that.

We spent our first night together in the grand and luxurious Providence Biltmore Hotel, one of the tallest buildings in Rhode Island at the time. The next day we took a train to New York City and spent the rest of my leave at a Manhattan hotel, followed by a week at the U.S. Army Air Forces base at Greensboro, North Carolina. Then we boarded a troop train to Victorville Army Air Field in the southern Mojave Desert. There was one little glitch in the trip. A GI named N.L. Billings was listed, with whoever was in charge of the manifold not realizing that N.L. Billings was a she. The car porter made the discovery the next morning and he, along with the rest of the GIs, scrambled for cover at the sight of a woman aboard. The porter handled the situation by taping a sign to one of the restrooms on which he had scrawled the word "Woman."

There was no dining car, so twice a day the train stopped at a town that had a restaurant and would wait until our designated time for eating had ended. At one such stop, the café was somewhat distant and we didn't hear the engine's whistle – in fact, we got back just in time to see a trail of smoke far ahead. So, we grabbed a taxi driver who said he could catch the train, and he did, after more than an hour's harrowing ride. On the sixth day, we got off at Victorville, where I would spend the next seven months on active duty working on the base, a B-24 maintenance facility.

For a week we lived on the second floor of the Victorville Hotel. There was no housing for married officers on base, but I was able to find a rental house in San Bernardino that we shared with another military pilot and his wife. There I bought a used car, a 1938 Chevy, and a pretty nice car, too. I had to drive sixty miles to the base in Victorville where I worked the swing shift from midnight until 8:00 a.m. After three months of this inconvenience, we rented a house in Wrightwood in the mountains at an elevation of about 5,000 feet. I had to drive down the mountain to get to the desert, which was about 3,000 feet above sea level. It cost me very little gas going down, but going up was a different story.

The community was popular for movie stars in the summertime. We met several celebrities (though I don't recall who they were – maybe not so famous after all!) who frequented the only café in town. Winters in the mountains were brutally cold and snowy, so we decided to move to the outskirts of Victorville where it was warmer and closer to the base. We rented an apartment shared with another tenant, which had a common bathroom with locks on both doors. The apartment was a former chicken coop owned by a farmer and his wife. The farmer had died, and his widow converted the coop into two one-bedroom apartments.

One morning as we were preparing breakfast, we were alarmed to see the wife running out with a broom chasing a cat. I rushed out and said, "Boy, do you have nerve!"

"What do you mean?"

I said, "You just chased off a bobcat!"

"What? I thought it was just an alley cat," she said, as her face drained its color.

During the winter, we couldn't get glycol antifreeze for the car – nobody could – almost all the production had been destined for the Air Force, which used glycol as a coolant for liquid-cooled airplanes like the P-51 and P-38. This left nothing for civilians. So, we had to use denatured alcohol in the radiator, but only at night. In the daytime we used water because the temperatures rose to a level that would cause the alcohol to boil off. Each night we drained the radiator, put the denatured alcohol in, and brought the hose in, too, so it wouldn't freeze. Then in the morning we'd drain the alcohol and pour water back in. It was a daily ritual.

On base, I was assigned as a deputy commander of one of the maintenance squadrons; in other words, it was a desk job. I would have never made a good desk job applicant or occupant, so the saving grace was that one of my responsibilities was to make sure that after an engine change or replacement or cylinder overhaul, the airplane went through a flight test. It was my job to arrange the three-man crew. I thought to myself, "Hmm. I'm responsible for arranging the crew, so, why can't I be the pilot?" That's what I did, and nobody said a word.

I was absent from that desk far more often than I sat behind it. The test flights were often overkill. For example, they might change the number three engine and a new engine would be installed that had to be airborne running. We'd go out, start up all four engines, taxi out, get ready for take-off, check each engine, taxi into position, put one, two and four through the wall with number three idling. Then we'd take off. The plane would be empty except for us three crew members and a few sandbags for weight and balance, usually way back in the tail.

After a short time, the flight engineer would fill in the blanks of the pages thick in his clipboard: time, airspeed height, oil temperature, and oil pressure. Then we'd advance to a minimum power, wait a period of time, and he'd put that down, then advance again, put it down. The last test to record was for a maximum of 1,000 horsepower for continuous operation. We'd run that for twenty minutes and write down the details. Putting her through all these permutations would take up to six hours and could be accomplished by circling the airport if I wanted to. Well, nothing would have been more boring (except sitting behind the desk). So, I took trips all over the place. One I especially enjoyed was the Grand Canyon. Having considerable experience in the Alps, it was nothing to zoom low through the canyon. Now, of course, I'd be put in jail if I tried something like that!

I'd fly out into the Mojave Desert with its sparse landscape and spindly, fragile Joshua trees. Back then, nobody thought to protect anything the way they do now. A full-grown man could walk up to one of those trees with its shallow roots and push the thing over, sort of like cow tipping. The wind often did just that. Today you can see some of the trees tethered for support. But at the time, I thought it would be fun to fly over and knock down a tree with the nose of my plane. People would sometimes ask me for a ride in the B-24. "Sure," I'd tell them. We'd be 1,000 feet over the desert. I'd say, "Would you like to go down and see what it looks like for a bombardier?" And I'd descend close to the ground and bump a Joshua tree. It was great fun.

Once, when I was killing time in the plane, a P-61 fighter called the Black Widow came whooshing right in front of us. This plane is faster than a B-24. I thought, "Maybe he wants to play!" So we played who can get on the other's tail. I got on his. The only thing he could do was go faster than me. He couldn't shake me off. I wish somebody had been on the ground making a movie that day. The B-24 was definitely not a fighter plane, but if you asked it to do that, it could. Another time I wondered, "How high can a B-24 really go?" With minimum weight of just us three crew members, I started climbing and ascended to 39,000 feet in an unpressurized airplane – and it flew! It was a little sloppy, but it flew. One weird thing happened and it was

Above: My childhood home. Bruce, my brother, still lives there.

Right: Almost two. My mother got the uniform wrong for an aviator-to-be!

Below: At the Jenkins Elementary School I was often in trouble for flying an airplane in my head instead of listening to my teacher.

Above left: My mother, Enid Alisca Bennett, was the creative spirit in our home. She loved big family gatherings. The stove in her kitchen never grew cold from her famous pies.

Above right: Brother Bruce and I are 17 years apart in age! (1939).

Below and opposite above: Happy memories of Scituate High and my close circle of friends. I would soon be leaving them to join the United States Army Air Corps.

Mom was initially opposed to my enlisting in the army but later changed her mind when she saw my gold bar and wings.

Above: After boot camp, I was selected for a special ancillary program at Syracuse College. My 90-day term there in early 1943 included 10 hours of flying time in a Taylor Cub, the best part of my college education!

Below left: I was designated driver in San Antonio during aviation cadet training, but it's not what you think! It's because I was the only cadet with a driver's license and the only one who could drive to the swimming pool when we had time off.

Below right: This is the Fairchild PT-19 used for training at Coleman Airfield, Texas, when I was there in the fall, 1943. It had no electricity and had to be hand-cranked. (Photo courtesy of Smithsonian National Air and Space Museum)

Home on leave to show off my shiny gold bar and wings. It was March 1944, the first time home since boot camp. Mom, Dad, sister Barbara, and little Bruce were kind of proud I'd made lieutenant.

She ain't pretty, but the B-24 Liberator had high cruise speed, long range, and capacity to hold up to 8,000 pounds in her two bomb bays. We called her the "Pregnant Pig."

The Charleston Army Air Field, South Carolina, is where my crew was assigned for bombing missions. We knew we'd make one helluva fighting machine.
First row, left to right: Dick Gottleber, Glen Sandberg and Warren Eldridge.
Second row, left to right: Me, Roland Nix and Charles "Smitty" Smith.

Above left: Toretta, also called Cerignola #3, was part of the Foggia Airfield complex in southern Italy, a strategic site for bombing missions into Europe and the Balkans. After a somewhat eventful trip across the Atlantic, I was ready for action.

Above right: Roland Nix, Warren Eldridge and I (right to left) adjust to tent living in Torretta as proud members of the 484th Bombardment Group of the 49th Bombardment Wing.

Left: The army kept Dick Gottleber and me supplied with ammo for target practice.

Six of our crew, including me, were reassigned in November 1944 to the 885th Heavy Special Bombardment Squadron of the Fifteenth Air Force in Brindisi, Italy. Later, we learned it was a front for the OSS. Pictured here are George Boyas (left), my radio operator, and a new tailgunner named Jim O'Flarity.

The B-24 got a makeover to equip her for secret OSS missions so she could fly undetected by the enemy. The olive drab was painted gloss black and polished. Other modifications, like the "Joe Hole," were made as well.

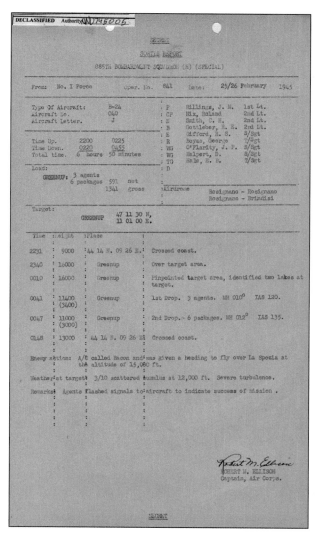

SECRET

SORTIE REPORT

885TH BOMBARDMENT SQUADRON (H) (SPECIAL)

From: No. I Force   Oper. No. 841   Date: 25/26 February 1945

Type Of Aircraft:	B-24	: P Billings, J. M. 1st Lt.
Aircraft No.	040	: CP Mix, Roland 2nd Lt.
Aircraft Letter.	J	: N Smith, C. H. 2nd Lt.
		: B Gottleber, R. E. 2nd Lt.
		: E Gifford, R. S. S/Sgt
Time Up. 2200 0225		: R Boyas, George T/Sgt
Time Down. 0220 0455		: WG O'Flarity, J. P. S/Sgt
Total time. 6 hours 50 minutes		: WG Halpert, D. S/Sgt
		: TG Hale, E. R. T/Sgt
Load:		: D
GREENUP: 3 agents		
6 packages 591 net		
1341 gross	:Airdrome Rosignano - Rosignano	
	Rosignano - Brindisi	

Target:

GREENUP   47 11 30 N,   11 01 00 E.

Time	Height	Place	
2231	9000	44 14 N. 09 26 E.	Crossed coast.
2340	16000	Greenup	Over target area.
0010	16000	Greenup	Pinpointed target area, identified two lakes at target.
0041	11400 (3400)	Greenup	1st Drop. 3 agents. MH 010° IAS 120.
0047	11000 (3000)	Greenup	2nd Drop. 6 packages. MH 012° IAS 135.
0148	13000	44 14 N. 09 26 E	Crossed coast.

Enemy action: A/C called Bacon and was given a heading to fly over La Spezia at the altitude of 15,060 ft.

Weather at target: 3/10 scattered cumulus at 12,000 ft. Severe turbulence.

Remarks: Agents flashed signals to aircraft to indicate success of mission.

Robert M. Ellison
ROBERT M. ELLISON
Captain, Air Corps.

SECRET

Left: Declassified sortie report for Operation Greenup, "by far the most successful of OSS operations" in southern Italy wrote William Casey, an OSS official who became head of the CIA.

Below: The real "Inglourious Basterds." Left to right: Franz Weber, Hans Wynbertt, and Fred Mayer. They made it safely to Oberperfuss, Austria, after the perilous drop from my B-24 to a frozen lake in the Alps.

Right: "Thrashed like a side of beef" by the Gestapo upon capture, OSS agent Fred Mayer never broke. He single-handedly negotiated the Nazi surrender of Innsbruck. Fred was the best friend I ever had until his death in April 2016.

Below: My crew was reassigned to Rosignano in March 1945 to be closer to the front lines south of Pisa, Italy. My last mission, "Slippery Yellow," was incomplete. By then, I had enough points to go home in May. The war was over and I was bound for America!

After leaving the military, I began my career as a commercial pilot. TWA recruited, then laid off pilots, including me. I was only too happy when Eastern hired me. It was a great ride with them from 1948 until mandatory retirement at age 60 in 1983.

Nancy and I were childhood sweethearts. We celebrated our 50th anniversary. She died six months later after battling cancer.

I receive frequent speaking requests, and during the Q&A after my talk at Seneca Ridge Middle School, of all things, they wanted to know the name of the wounded magpie that was our tent companion in Italy.

Barbara and I married in 1997, 38 years after meeting on a flight to Savannah, Georgia, in the Martin 404. She was the flight attendant and I the gaga-eyed pilot.

In 2002, Barbara and I went with the 484th Bomb Group to Italy to see if we could find remnants of the old Torretta air base. This is a piece of the Marston Mat that had been used for the runway.

The Quonset hut had been our maintenance hanger.

Above: Rusting hangar of
the 484th Bomb Group.

Left: One of the
deteriorating buildings
on site.

Nevin Showman, my
close friend and Angel
Flight partner, knows
just about everything
I know about flying. Like
me, he finds great reward
in combining his love of
flying with his love of
people.

This adorable little girl asked me, "If I'm going on an Angel Flight, does that mean I'm an angel?" Naturally, I confirmed it. By the end of the flight, both of us were absolutely convinced!

Diana was our special cargo for a double mission from Richmond to Baltimore for her treatment and then her return home. We always give our passengers a traveling companion that never fails to bring a smile.

Angel Flight West annually presents their distinguished Endeavor Award, and I was one of the lucky ones to be given it in May 2015.

Our historic flight around America in 2015 covered 5,758 nautical miles and 13 days of flight.

Above: Returning to Victorville 70 years later was the biggest thrill of our journey and very emotional for me. It is where I'd overseen maintenance of the B-24s stored on the base after the war.

Left: We received a royal welcome back home in Virginia. The support throughout the trip was overwhelming. My next bucket list wish is to fly around the world in a Pilatus (waiting for my sponsor).

Our reminiscences brought both laughs and tears at Fred Mayer's (left) 80th birthday party in 2001. For the celebration, he invited his fellow Greenup team members to Harper's Ferry, West Virginia. Next to Fred is Jim O'Flarity, myself, and Dick Gottleber. Franz Weber and Hans Wynbert came too. It's impossible to put into words the depth of feeling we shared at this unforgettable reunion.

Another happy get-together with Fred in 2003. His death in 2016 was an immense loss. He was my best friend and hero.

Barbara, with considerable help from Nevin and Sharon Showman, pulled a fast one on me. They threw a surprise party at my hangar at Luray Caverns airport in Virginia (KLUA), to celebrate my 95th birthday. Three of my Eastern Airlines pilot buddies joined the surprise. What a celebration!

Nostalgic moment in the cockpit of an old B-24. This was on exhibit at the 484th Bombardment Group reunion in Dayton, Ohio, September 2018.

because of the lack of pressure. I sort of sucked on my tongue, and it felt like it was going to come out! Man, did that ever scare me! When I recall that flight back in August of 1945, I find it interesting to consider that I went through my entire professional flying career without ever exceeding the altitude I'd reached in my B-24; that is until after I'd retired and was traveling on a 747 that went up to 41,000 feet in a pressurized cabin.

Another adventure I had in Victorville was flying over those celebrities' summer homes down in the canyons. I thought it would be fun to fly over my place, too. At 13,000 feet I looked down and saw someone in our yard who I figured was Nancy. I reached over and ran the props up and back, up and back. This made an echoing roar as I went lower and lower, then quickly ascended. I happened to glance over at the co-pilot and flight engineer and noticed they were laughing. "Is this a private joke?" I asked.

"No, we loved your buzz job," they said.

That was the wrong thing to say to someone who'd been in the OSS and typically flew less than 100 feet off the ground – and at night. By then, I'd learned the typography of the entire area, so I just flew southeast, slowly, not saying anything. I flew up near Lake Arrowhead, a famous hunting and fishing resort on top of a mountain that in ancient times had blown its top off, creating a bowl. There were higher mountains to the west, and to the east, a gentle slope. The lake's surface was around 8,000 feet. I let the airplane come down right over the trees. "I smell fumes," I told the engineer. "Would you go back to the bomb bay and crack the doors open a little bit?" This was common for the B-24.

At the base of the bomb bay catwalk is a small antenna for the ADF, which stands for automatic direction finding. I came down nice and smooth, put the antenna in the water, and made a spray. It so happened there were two guys fishing in a boat a little way off, and all I could see was their eyeballs. Next, I headed toward what appeared to be impenetrable cliffs. The co-pilot's mouth dropped. "Uh, uh, uhm."

I wasn't through. I gently pulled the nose up until I was maybe fifty feet off the water. I reached up, shut off all four engines, and pulled it up sharply, then turned. If you had looked down on it, you would have seen that the exit of the lake went into a granite wall, with more wall behind it, but I just climbed without power and let the plane slide down the hill, down into the Redman area of California. Then I put the power back up so he could finish his calculations and said, "What was that about a buzz job?"

One day, I got a call from a representative from the Federal Aviation Administration offering me a civilian pilot's license because of my wartime service. Now, during this point in my career, I'd come to a crossroads and was toying with the idea of staying in the service. This gave me two choices. I could accept a tour of duty in the army reserves or choose to be a career soldier. If I went into the reserves, I'd keep my commission. This was attractive; as a captain, my paycheck was pretty decent. The only problem, as I soon found out, was that mine was a wartime commission and, with the war over and the military cutting back, the commission was only temporary. If I stayed in the military as a career soldier, I'd be a sergeant, with a third of the pay I'd been getting. Well, that didn't seem like a hard question. I decided to take the reserve and do something civilian. The FAA offer looked like the perfect opportunity, except for one thing: Nancy. For some reason, I got the idea that she didn't want me to fly anymore. Maybe it was something she said, or perhaps I took it the wrong way. At any rate, I turned down the chance to have a civilian pilot license and resolved that my flying days were over.

I loved math and science and I was good at them, so I decided to go back to school. Nancy and I packed up the Chevy and headed east. One thing you couldn't buy back then was a new tire because rubber had gone to the war. We lost two tires before even getting out of California! We had to scrounge around in the next little town, Barstow, near the Nevada border. The service station owner took pity on us. "Sorry, I don't have a tire that fits but that's alright. Hang on. I'll go see if this other fella has one." He got in his car and drove off, then returned a short while later with a new tire. We drove on Route 66 as far as it went, somewhere near St. Louis, then continued on to New England.

Nancy and I bunked in the attic of my folks' house in Scituate as we looked for a house of our own. I applied to MIT and checked out books to study from the library across the street, the same library I'd frequented in school when I borrowed books on electronics and trigonometry. After brushing off the dust from my head, I went to Cambridge and took the entrance exam, scoring a ninety-six-overall average. I was pretty proud of that. I was all set to start at MIT and pursue electrical engineering, but it would have to be a five-year program instead of four. This meant paying tuition for five long years and taking fewer classes per day since I had to work to support Nancy with a baby on the way. I got a job in Cohasset, the next town over, as a machine operator making parts for Raytheon. There were several weeks before school started and in the interim I ran into some old friends who hadn't qualified for military service because of medical reasons. They were graduate engineers at MIT and had gone through the four-year course.

"How much are you guys making?" I asked, wanting some idea of what to expect for myself.

"Forty a week," they said. Now forty dollars a week was worth more back then and would give you a livelihood but nothing much more than that. It seemed like a dead end to me. On the way home, my thoughts were swarming. "I'm doing this because Nancy didn't want me to fly. But that's all I've ever really wanted to do. This program is going to take five years! And we have one in the oven! I'm putting my foot down!" As soon as I got home, I marched into the bedroom and without giving her so much as a chance to say hello, I said, "I'm going to give up the school. I'm going to pursue flying and a career in aviation!"

She was sitting on the side of the bed combing her hair and looked at me curiously. "Well, I always wondered why you didn't."

My mouth dropped open. "But I thought you didn't want me to fly."

"I don't know what gave you that idea. You must have misunderstood something I said."

Since the opportunity of having a free license was gone, I had to enroll in flying school and go through the motions of starting from scratch. It was all easy and fun and paid for by the GI Bill. The East Coast Aviation Corporation operated two small schools, one in the headquarters at the Providence Airport (Rhode Island) and the other in Bedford, Massachusetts, which is where Nancy and I were going to settle. I guess they liked the way I flew, so I went ahead and got all my ratings, including instructor, both flight and ground. The planes were single and twin engine, almost like toys compared to the B-24! My training took all of the summer of 1946. It was also during that summer that our first child, Susan Lee, was born. (Two others would follow, Leslie, another daughter, born in 1951; and Lee, our son, in 1953.)

The company offered me a position as a flight instructor, and I was able to teach at the school in Bedford, where they needed a ground instructor. Five teachers were employed there, including myself, but I was the only ground instructor. As a flight instructor I taught only one person. As a ground instructor, I taught the whole school. The pay was $2.50 an hour. I was able to buy a house for $9,000 on a GI Bill housing loan, a little two-bedroom ranch in Woburn, Massachusetts, located two towns away from Bedford. I was still working as a machine operator and still commuting.

By the second year of instructing, I'd acquired enough students to teach full-time and no longer needed the hassle of working at the machine shop, so I resigned. Bedford at that time was both a commercial and USAAF airport. Whenever I had a break, I'd walk about fifty paces and go fly one of the reserve airplanes, a nice enough form of recreation. A group of students from MIT had formed a small aero club and bought a Cessna 120. It was a tail-dragger with two seats side by side and a motor with sixty-five horsepower. There was no electricity aboard. Even though Bedford had a tower, it was also equipped for non-radio operations using light signals.

The club decided they wanted me as their instructor. They kept the plane at the school because it provided a tie-down, maintenance, and other benefits. The next thing I knew, they were asking me to teach at MIT and explained that the club had been granted authorization to use a classroom one night a week. "We need a ground instructor," they explained, and I agreed immediately. There were probably ten to twenty members of the aero club in class. In those days, the big device was an E6B. This was an aviation calculator – a circular slide rule. It was manually operated to solve wind triangles and so forth. It was very handy and solved problems automatically. These were engineering students. Every one of them had a conventional slide rule but they didn't want to buy an E6B or anything else, so I had to show them how to use their mathematical slide rules to solve aviation-related problems. Not such a bad thing to be an MIT professor at age twenty-four and not even have a college degree! However, my career as a reservist in the military was an entirely different matter.

To maintain reserve status, you had to put in a certain number of hours and go on a two-week bivouac. You also had to attend a weekly evening lecture, which I did. One day, the colonel said, "One of the requirements here is that you show up in uniform – the blue uniform." When the National Security Act of 1947 created the U.S. Air Force and its reserve component, the Air National Guard, the change in name required a new uniform. As an officer, I was supposed to buy it. But as a new father and homeowner, I had very little discretionary money, and the cost of the uniform – around $270 – was definitely beyond my budget. And that's what brought my military career to an end.

Chapter 12

TWA

Trans World Airlines was hiring. To apply, I had to go to LaGuardia in New York and take a test. I walked into a large room crowded with people, pilots, and co-pilots from other airlines. "Wow, the competition is fierce!" I thought. I took the test, which included weird psychological questions that had nothing to do with flying, and fortunately I scored high enough to be accepted. At that time, TWA was hiring everyone they could and filling a class each month with at least thirty people. But suddenly, the word came down from TWA higher-ups asking, "So, where's the increase in air traffic?"

It seems the vice president of operations had foreseen a tremendous boom in air travel, but he was a little myopic. That surge didn't come for a long time. Turns out there *was* no increase, which meant TWA had to start cutting back – to the tune of 600 people! I was in the last class to go through before the cutoff, so my job was secure, at least for the time being. The company sent me to Kansas City for a month of ground school, mostly to learn company procedures and practice instrument approaches. The rest was academic, learning weather, traffic, how the company wanted to be perceived, and so forth. I was flying TWA's DC-3, a plane without quirks and with old technology, but it did what was asked of it. It could seat twenty-one passengers and had the same Pratt and Whitney engine as the B-24, but in many ways the B-24 was far more advanced with its electronics and navigation.

During training, my plane, which we flew all around the airport and the Kansas City area, was somewhat uncomfortable and had a complicated steam heating system for warming the cabin. Before landing at an airport with temperatures below freezing, the co-pilot would have to leave his seat and position the valves near the boiler. These were mounted just behind him in such a manner as to trap all the water from the heater shroud around the right engine's exhaust pipes. With all these valves, pipes, and wheels, it was like looking into an old-fashioned steam train. If the co-pilot didn't do his job and have everything shut down by the time we landed, ice would form and break the pipes.

I began my new career at the TWA base in Boston. But the company was still looking for ways to cut employees, and I knew I could be next. My seniority was established with the date of hire – August 1, 1948 – and if that matched someone else's date of hire, then the oldest person was assigned the highest number. I was the lowest, only sixth from the end of the whole list of around 1,200. The way they tried to weed out the weakest was to give a check ride every time you flew. For an entire year, the command pilot nitpicked, saying, for example, "John, do you know the name of the town right below?"

"Yes, that's Corydon, Indiana."

"That's the wrong answer," he said.

I looked again. "See the racetrack on the south end of town and the railroad track going northwest through town? That's Corydon."

"You weren't listening, were you? What did I ask you?"

"You wanted to know the name of the town." I was getting seriously annoyed.

"No, I didn't. I said *do you know* the name of the town? There's only two answers you could have given, yes or no. If you'd answered yes, I might have asked you what the name of the town was."

When it was time to change seats, I'd taxi out, then wait to be cleared for take-off. He'd say, "Okay, I'll line it up while you put up the hood." The hood was a black enclosure that made nothing visible except the instrument panel. I had to make an instrument take-off every single time and didn't actually see the ground until I'd reached minimum altitude, even on a bright, sunny day. It was good practice. I knew they were trying to get rid of employees and that the captains had no choice. They had to file a report on every trip. With TWA, the whole twelve months I was there was basically one long check ride. I didn't let it piss me off. Interestingly enough, one of the captains, Arthur Sessi, who'd nearly nitpicked me to death, became a close friend, and our families often got together. With my encouragement, he built himself a Heath kit television, and I built him a mahogany cabinet. I flew often with Arthur, right up to the end of my short-lived TWA career.

The company's upper echelon was saying they absolutely couldn't handle the overload of employees and demanded that thirty people be cut every month. Everybody that was left of the more recent hires got laid off, including me. Once again, I was facing an unknown future and left Boston, wondering what was next.

Chapter 13

Skies and Scrapes

I called several other airlines looking for a position, but the answer was always negative. Eastern was a company that appealed to me, so when I was in Providence visiting my in-laws, I called their New York base. "Sorry, there are no openings, and if there were, I've got a list that would fill up a roll of toilet paper." So, I figured, *that's off.*

To my amazement, I got a call two days later from Eastern Airlines in Miami, asking if I'd like to come and work for them. One of the other TWA pilots had gone to Miami directly, presented himself, and gotten hired. The Eastern guy told me that the chief pilot in Kansas City had a list of pilots who'd gotten laid off and said to call him if he needed other pilots. So, that's how my name came up. I barely had time to breathe out an emphatic *yes* when the guy says, "Okay, I want you to be down here on Monday morning, ready for ground school."

He sent a telegraph to the Providence airport telling them I would be getting a free ride to Miami. I arrived on a Sunday, found a room to rent, and went to my first day of ground school at Eastern on Monday morning. There were four of us; it turns out we'd all worked for TWA. Before long, a man not much older than me and with a casual smile, walks in. "I'm your new ground instructor," he says. "I understand that you've all worked for an airline before, so I want each of you to tell us about it."

We all told the same story, how we'd worked for TWA, trained, got bumped.

"Sounds like you got a whole lot of training in, didn't you? Well, it's time we went and got a bite to eat." It was 10:00 a.m., and we figured we'd all be going to a cafeteria or something. "I'll drive," he said, and off we went in his car to Miami Beach, where we ate, hangar-talked, and looked out on turquoise sea and white sand. The other pilots and I had been issued a company manual. "I expect it's going to be easy for you to consume that," our instructor said. "We'll talk about it tomorrow."

The next day, he asked a few questions about the manual, then said, "Time to go get a bite," and drove us back to the beach. The morning after that, he made a speech and said, "Doesn't look like you need any more training. I think you're probably going to enjoy flying for Eastern. Oh, and sign this paper." We signed it, a simple statement like, "I agree to the terms of employment for Eastern Airlines." Afterward, he told us we could go back home. "Somebody will call you and tell you where you're going to be based."

A week later, I got a call that I was to go to Chicago. I would be flying a DC-3 again, but this one had a bona fide heater. Eastern was a smaller airline but the company offered more job security. My number at hiring was in the 600s. They also had routine training and a philosophy very different from TWA's obsession with minutiae. Eastern was more liberal and fun to work for. Everyone was friendly and laid back. In fact, one time I came to work and a captain I'd never met before says, "You're one of those TWA guys, right?" I nodded. "Well, I'm sick of flying. You can fly today." And so I flew all day, even though technically I wasn't really a person for eighteen months since I could be terminated for any reason.

Every six months we'd go down to Miami for training, all of it in the airplane (simulators hadn't yet been invented). One of the elements of the procedures was a minimum descent altitude. Based on when he's able to see the runway or not, the pilot decides either to land or declare a missed approach. In aviation, you have both a precision and non-precision approach. The latter is typically a radio-range approach in places where there are no obstructions. ILS (Instrument Landing System) is the precision approach. For that we trained to go down to 50 feet instead of the standard 200 feet minimum. The idea was that if you can go down to 50 feet on a precision approach, you can easily go down to 200 feet. For a non-precision approach, if you can manage 100 feet you can certainly manage 400 feet.

One morning, we showed up early at Chicago Midway airport and got to talking to a captain who was flying a DC-4. He happened to be the check pilot (the chief pilot over us). Both my plane and his were headed to Atlanta, only he was leaving later than ours and was flying direct to Nashville and then to Atlanta. My captain and I, on the other hand, had several stops before reaching our final destination in Atlanta. We went from Chicago to Indianapolis, then to Louisville, Chattanooga, and Nashville. At every stop, we landed below limits, and when it was my turn to bring the plane down in Nashville, I was probably no more than fifty feet above the ground. I saw the runway, landed, and taxied in.

Just before we shut down the engine, I heard the voice of the check captain on the DC-4 entering the realm and being directed to the outer marker. I'm thinking, "Oh, my God, my captain's going to get in trouble because they'll see we came in below minimums." I got out and nervously walked to the office. Just as I swung the door open, I looked back and here's the DC-4 coming in below minimums just like I did and touching down. The captain and co-pilot strode in, threw up a hand to say hello, and started talking as if everything was just as it should be. That was Eastern for you.

When I first started working there, I heard a true story about a brand-new co-pilot. On the first day of training, he got to the airport three hours ahead of schedule, memorized the weather, tore off teletypes, and did all the preliminary things he was supposed to do. After a couple of hours he went to the flight line but didn't see the captain anywhere. So, he figured he'd go out and check over the airplane. He walked all around it, checking this and that, made sure the fuel was on board, then went up in the cockpit. Still no captain. The new guy was patient. Five minutes before departure time, the captain shows up, sits down, looks out the window, and turns to the co-pilot. "Start two" was all he said, and off they went.

On the second trip, the guy says to himself, "I really don't have to get there three hours early – maybe two is enough." So he did the same thing as before, memorized the weather, tore off the teletypes, did a walkaround of the plane. Once again, the captain didn't show up until five minutes before departure. On the third trip, the passengers were all on board when the new guy and the captain showed up and were trying to get into the cockpit at the same time. The captain says, "Did you check the weather?"

The co-pilot says, "Why? We're going anyway!" That, too, was Eastern!

On one occasion, I was flying a freighter with a cargo of 50,000-day-old chickens. Freighters flew all night. We were in a holding pattern over Louisville. It was 3:00 a.m. and calm. The captain turned to me and said, "Have you ever made a Zero Zero yet?" (That's a landing where you can't see anything. The ceiling and visibility are both zero.)

"No, not yet."

"Would you like to?"

"Yes, sir," I said.

When we reached the minimum of 200 feet, we got into fog and zero visibility both downward and ahead. Zero Zero.

"Here's what we'll do," says the captain. "I want you to make it nice and smooth. Slowly dissipate your speed to landing speed. When you hit the top, then you just absolutely nail the cross." This was a reference to the meter that shows whether you're up or on or below the glide path. It also shows if you're right or left of the track. That was easy enough to do, especially in calm conditions. "I'll look out the front window and as soon as I see the runway, you'll feel my hands on the wheel," he said.

Everything was working out, and the speed was ever so slow, weaning away. I kept waiting for the feel on the wheel but it didn't come. But I did feel the bump on the wheels, so I made sure I kept the airplane going straight ahead until it stopped. But then came a problem when the captain, who was on tower frequency, says, "We're on the ground, but we've run into a big fog bank." Of course, he wasn't admitting that he knew about the fog from 200 feet altitude! It was a touchy thing taxiing to the freight terminal. We had to taxi very slowly to see where the lights were. But we made it. Then the cargo handlers unloaded what was destined for Louisville – those thousands of smelly chickens - and loaded what was destined for St. Louis. It was just breaking dawn when we left.

Eastern was a great company to work for and ahead of its time. It was the first airline to have ILS minimums of 200-foot ceiling minimum and a half mile forward visibility. There was a period in Newark where fifty-four Eastern airplanes took off when none of the other airlines were flying. For business travel, everyone knew Eastern was the one to go on, and we had many regulars. The service was above and beyond. Sometimes we'd have an unaccompanied child whose flight was delayed and who missed the next trip. In such cases the ramp agent would take the child home to his or her own house.

For the first eighteen months with Eastern, co-pilots were assigned to captains (the same applied to TWA, but of course I was there for only a year). You couldn't be assigned to the same captain for more than ninety days in a row. This was probably in case you and he didn't get along. The high-paying trips were those that extended into the after-midnight period. Co-pilots got a salary, unlike captains, who were paid by the hour. For the first six months with Eastern, I earned $165 per month. The second six months, I got a forty-dollar raise. A couple of years later, the co-pilots negotiated a contract so they were able to get the hourly rate as well. For eighteen months, I flew with senior captains. I spent six months in Chicago and lived in a room in a lodging house on the southside so Nancy could come for visits.

My next assignment was New York City. For nearly a year, Nancy, Susan, and I lived in an apartment in Queens Village. In January of 1950, I rented a Levittown house in Nassau County for all of sixty-five dollars a month. William J. Levitt was the first mass housing producer, and his company,

Levitt & Sons, built affordable tract houses after the war when so many GIs were coming home and raising families. Now, they sell for $400,000 and more. Our house had two bedrooms, a living room, bathroom, kitchen, and an attic. Levittown houses were built on slabs embedded with piping heated by the furnace. In the winter the floors were nice and toasty. I used the attic for my shop and built a saw table for woodworking. In fact, I still have one of the tables that I made those many years ago.

Our next move was to Hicksville, Long Island, where I bought a house of our own. This town is where both our daughter, Leslie, and our son, Lee, were born. It seemed like the end of the world. We had to drive a good distance to the grocery store. During the eight and a half years we lived there, Manhattan had crept up on us and continued its never-ending sprawl. In August 1962, I put in a bid for a position in Washington, D.C., and won it, but the deadhead commute got old quickly. For six months I made that trip. It was hard on me and my family, so I decided to relocate.

We moved to historic Mt. Vernon, Virginia. I bought a spacious, colonial-styled home located on what had been George Washington's property. A real estate magnate, he had owned thousands of acres of land in that area. We lived at 4101 Nellie Custis Court for the rest of my career with Eastern, which spanned a little over thirty-four years and ended in August 1983. FAA regulations at the time called for pilots to retire at age sixty. Now it's age sixty-five, with no age limitations on private pilots.

I flew several different airplanes for Eastern, beginning as a co-pilot with the DC-3. I made it my job to teach myself the intricacies of that airplane just as I had learned the B-24. In fact, I got to know every airplane I flew, inside and out. I used to go down to maintenance at LaGuardia and into their archive machine to print out diagrams, specs, and so forth. I flew the DC-3, DC-4, and the sleek, propeller-driven Constellation, affectionally called the "Connie." I flew the Martin 404 as a co-pilot and then as a captain when I achieved that rank in 1955. My favorite plane was the DC-9, which I flew from 1969 until my retirement in 1983. It had the most reserve power of any airplane I've ever flown. You could fill it up at the gate in Atlanta, taxi out to the runway, get cleared for take-off, shut off one of the engines, and continue the take-off from a standing still position. Of course, that wouldn't be a good thing to do, but that's what the DC-9 has the capacity to do – 28,000 pounds of thrust!

One thing I enjoyed about my position as a captain was being able to handle panicky passengers. I had final say in most matters, which I utilized – and often creatively. But gate agents had to rigidly follow rules. One memorable incident involving a husband and wife required an innovative solution. The couple had been pre-boarded, and the wife was terribly agitated due to her husband's medical condition. Eastern's policy was that when a passenger needed oxygen, as this man did, Eastern would supply it. The husband wanted to use his own oxygen mask because the airline one was extremely uncomfortable. The inflexible agent, wanting to board the rest of the passengers, insisted the man use Eastern's mask. One of the flight attendants stuck her head inside the cockpit and said to me, "Maybe you should come back and help out here." I went immediately to the cabin and slipped into the seat row in front of them, then turned to face them with my arms on the back of the seat.

"What's your concern?" I asked.

"I want him to use his own mask," the wife said, her voice wavering.

"Here, let me look at it."

The agent stood there, stalwart and locked in place. "He's going to do it just like the company says," I thought. "This is a one-use mask, isn't it?" I said to him.

"Yes, it is."

I reached in my pocket and pulled out my trusty knife, made one clean cut and handed him back the airline mask.

"Now, as you can see, we're using the hose supplied by the company," I said, then pushed it on to the man's mask. "Try that," I said, and he did. Problem solved, couple relieved, agent wide-eyed.

Another incident that stretched both skill and judgment occurred when I was flying the Martin 404 and based in New York. This would have been around 1957. The trip was to Burlington, Vermont, with stops in Albany and Saranac Lake, a village in the Adirondacks in upstate New York. With good weather, as it was the day of my near disaster, we were legal to fly using Visual Flight Rules (VFR). This meant we flew direct instead of going out of our way, as we had to do on Instrument Flight Rules (IFR), so we landed at the airport half an hour ahead of schedule. I taxied to the terminal and swung around so the plane's back end was close to the building. Rear steps came out from under the tail allowing the passengers to exit. There to oversee everything was Johnny Campe, Eastern's jack of all trades, who was a combination ticket seller, ramp agent, baggage handler, and passenger-complaint department. (The actual airport manager hardly ever showed up, even though he was on the payroll.) Johnny was a delight to be around and funny as hell. Everything was always fine with him – good weather or bad, it didn't matter.

After the passengers got off and while the "ground crew" (the gasoline truck driver) was unloading baggage, I stepped out of the plane and looked around.

"Hey, John!" somebody said and waved in my direction. On the other side of the ramp was a little Cessna and standing beside it was one of the captains who lived in the area. I've forgotten his name, so I'll just call him Bob.

"Well, hello," I said, and we chatted for a bit. Bob told me he'd been in a ski accident during the winter and broken his leg. In order to fly, he had to have another pilot, who happened to be the gas truck driver. Since he couldn't use his leg to push the rudder, he'd rigged up a small rod that he could operate by hand.

"Hey, you've got time, don't you? Let's go for a little ride in my airplane."

At that time, I'd never flown a Cessna. Now I own a Cessna 172RG. ("RG" stands for retractable gear.) Not one to turn down a chance to fly, I said, "Okay," and jumped in.

"Just twist the key and it will start." And it did.

There were three runways, so I asked him which one he wanted to use.

"Go take off to the west."

I taxied out toward the end of twenty-seven, the westerly runway, but Bob interrupted me. "Oh, you can take off from here with this little airplane." There was no way either of us could have foreseen the consequences of his decision. I pushed the throttle in and felt the airplane. Pretty soon, it felt like it wanted to fly, and sure enough it did. We began to climb, and I saw the gleam of Lake Saranac below. The wind was calm, and I was enjoying my first flight in a Cessna when all of a sudden, everything got quiet – real quiet. The engine had stopped!

Well, there was no sense in looking around in the cockpit, because I wasn't familiar with it. I had no idea what was happening or why. So, I went back to the primary rule: above all, fly the airplane! I could tell I was too low to turn and go on another runway, so I was going to have to go straight ahead. There wasn't enough runway left. "Well," I thought, "I'll just have to take my risks and go into the scrubby pine trees ahead." I kept the nose high and flew as slow as possible to minimize any damage.

In the meantime, as I was later to be told, my co-pilot in the Martin had gone to the back of the plane to chat with the flight attendant, who was sweet on him. Johnny Campe came up and said, "I bet you don't know where your captain is right now!"

"I left him in the cockpit," said the co-pilot.

"Oh, no. He's not in the cockpit. He's right there!" As he spoke, Johnny threw up his hand and pointed to the Cessna. It was at that precise moment that the engine quit, and the three of them watched with jaws dropped.

"Oh, my God, what am I going to do? I've gotta call dispatch. What am I gonna tell them? Cancel the trip because the captain had a crash?"

Now, back to me in the airplane. I could see out of the corner of my eye that Bob was doing something or other in the cockpit and checking things out. We were down within five feet of the ground. The scrubby little pine trees were coming up fast, but I don't think we would have gotten hurt. The airplane might have gotten damaged, but I think Bob and I would have been okay.

"Well, damn him!" Bob exclaimed, then moved his hand to make an adjustment. All of a sudden, the engine roared into life and we leaped into the air. Of course, I'd left the throttle wide open the whole time.

"What happened?"

"Looks like the gas man thought I was going to put the airplane away for the night, so he shut off the fuel tank yesterday. There was enough leftover fuel in the carburetor and fuel line to get us to that point before it quit."

Now that we were safe and sound, we decided to keep going on our little adventure. We flew all around the lake, and he showed me where he lived, what this or that place was, and then we returned to the airport, right on time for departure. I got in the Martin 404 and was greeted with words of relief and amazement by my crew. With the passengers comfortably seated, away we went, across the lake and on to Burlington. It was a great day for flying.

Chapter 14

Fuel-saving Magic

One of the most important benefits I bequeathed to Eastern during my career was the accidental discovery that I could save the company tens of thousands of dollars on fuel. Only trouble is, the company looked the gift horse in the mouth. In 1971, I took off from Nassau in the DC-9 en route to New York. I filed my flight plan with the controller, and they assigned me an altitude of 33,000 feet. On take-off, I changed from tower to departure control.

As I was climbing, the controller pointed out potential conflicting traffic ahead and asked if I could see the plane. I could not. The controller had us hold at 4,000 feet until clear of traffic. I happened to notice that our speed was 380 knots, or 437 miles per hour. This speed exceeded the maximum of 365 knots. An air speed indicator was supposed to give a warning alarm if the speed went over the limit, but the alarm never went off. I figured it wasn't working, so I reduced my speed to 365 while maintaining the holding altitude. Soon, the controller contacted us and said we were clear of traffic and for us to resume the climb to the assigned altitude of 33,000. I pulled the nose up gradually so I wouldn't alarm the passengers by a sudden pitch change. I could have reduced the power but didn't because I figured the airplane would slow down.

Pretty soon I'm going up like a rocket, but the instrument still showed we were at maximum speed. "What's going on?" I wondered. I continued to monitor it and keep the plane at maximum speed. We arrived at altitude considerably sooner than if we had been using the recommended climb speed, which was quite a bit lower. For some unknown reason, we used far less fuel and had a faster climb rate on that trip than what the computer had calculated for maximum efficiency.

This got me thinking. I started following the accidental procedures deliberately, and the results were predictable. I could get to altitude sooner and faster, and literally pass up traffic. Still mystified by this phenomenon,

I started keeping records. Of course, I'd long since found out that the airplane was a fantastic glider, so I added that to my procedures and on my descent, put the plane in a glide much sooner than Eastern's recommendations. I kept raw data records for six months, which took us into the winter. I didn't attempt to modify it for any of the delays or other variations. I kept the records of all the computerized flight plans and recommended procedures for each trip. On the computer's flight plan, every single one had a line at the bottom saying, "This flight plan was calculated as if you were the only airplane in the sky. Consider that and apply reserves." The inference was that in the real world you couldn't even make the trip on the fuel calculated by the computer.

The average over six months turned out to be 80,000 pounds per month (that was just one pilot, one trip, one crew). At that time the average cost of jet fuel was ten cents a pound. Therefore, they were saving $8,000 a month on my trips. "Wait till I tell this to the company!" I thought with excitement.

So, I wrote letters, and many of them. One day, I received an invitation to headquarters in Miami to meet with the vice president of operations, the company navigator (whose job it was to put all the information into the computer), and the company meteorologist (who reported atmospheric conditions that might affect the efficiency of the aircraft) to present my fuel-saving claim. I had a suitcase full of papers – maybe twenty-five pounds' worth – with all the data I'd collected to verify my claims. Right off, I got this pointed question: "What do you have a degree in, anyway?" I said that I had not completed college but had attended for only three months. Their response: "Okay, we'll research this matter."

In a month or so, I got a letter from Douglas Aircraft Company, which boiled down to this: "No, the DC-9 can't do that."

"Well, I'm doing it. It's happening," I said to no one in particular. "And I don't care if I have a formula for saving fuel or not!" The fact is, I was arriving at my destination before the computer said I could and was using considerably less fuel. Of course, I also utilized the gliding capabilities of the DC-9. Typically, I would close the power levers to flight idle 150 miles from destination and wouldn't touch the power again until after it was on the ground to get to the gate. That was the routine.

I had another rabbit to pull out of my hat to increase efficiency, and that was my handheld HP-45 calculator. The device was programmable, making it one of the most advanced calculators of the time. I wrote a program for it that I called RNav, for Area Navigation, and it allowed me to fly direct from any place to any place with perfect accuracy. The DC-9 didn't have this capability. Once on a trip in the DC-9 nonstop from Tampa to Chicago, my co-pilot and I were nearing O'Hare when we heard reports of a storm. We got into a holding pattern because of traffic and were slowing, making our descent.

When it came my turn to make the approach IFR, the controller said, "There's nobody in front of you now. I could go ahead and let you make your approach. However, the holding stacks all around us are filled with missed approaches."

"Tell me," I said quickly, "who was the last one that made a go-around?" He said it was an Eastern 727 and that the description of flying on the final approach was, "Violent."

"Never mind, we won't do it," I said. "I want an immediate clearance to our alternate, Indianapolis."

"You got it."

"I want 16,000 feet." This was the altitude I needed for fuel savings.

I switched radio contact from tower to company and reported what I was doing.

"That's okay," said the dispatcher, "but I don't know how you're able to fly there. My computations show that you don't have any fuel. And, at Indianapolis there's only one runway left open. If somehow you had enough fuel to get to Louisville, there's nobody on Louisville." I made a quick calculation and called Standiford Field in Louisville to ask if there were any delays going in.

"No delays whatsoever. We're very light."

"Okay, I'm coming in," I said, then notified ATC that we were going to Louisville. "I want to be clear to climb as high as I want," I told the controller, "until I take the power off and descend and do all of that without asking you again."

"Okay, we have you in the radar contact. Do what you want to do."

I told the co-pilot to go to maximum speed and power, and to climb as long as I said so. He did exactly that, and at the point I had calculated where the plane should be, I said, "Close the throttles now," and he shut off the engines. Then I told him to go to the airspeed I'd previously figured out as the best glide speed to use. He did that. We landed safely in Louisville, and with an hour of fuel left over at that! The co-pilot, who'd never flown with me before, was impressed with my procedure. We refueled, and, learning that the storm had passed, flew to Chicago. All the airplanes that had been scattered to outlying fields were still tied up on the ground, but we went in with no trouble at all.

One time they sent the assistant chief pilot of Washington on the jump seat with me to see what I was doing. As it happened on that trip, I didn't get the climb rate – clearly something was wrong. I sent the co-pilot back through the cabin, telling him, "Look out on the wings and let me know what you see."

He came back and said, "The speed brakes are up an inch and a half." (Speed brakes are flap-like things that come up on top of the wing to allow you to go down fast without increasing speed.) Apparently, this airplane was out of rig, but unfortunately, it substantiated the company's position that my plan didn't work – quite a blow indeed.

There was one occasion where I *did* manage to impress someone from Eastern. Twice a year a company check pilot would be scheduled to ride along with each pilot to make sure he was doing the right thing. One day they sent a fellow I knew very well. He lived about four houses away from me at Mt. Vernon. He got on and introduced himself formally.

"Okay, Bill," I said. "Do you want me to show you that I know what the rules and procedures are? Would you like to see how I fly this airplane?"

"Sure. Why don't you show me how you fly?"

So I did. The trip was from Washington National to Atlanta. At the end, we had to make an instrument approach. We had a little bit of holding to do but soon landed and taxied to the gate. I told the co-pilot to give Bill the computer flight plan. He looked at the fuel totalizer (the instrument that records how much fuel you use and reads out on the panel). It was 1,200 pounds less than the theoretical minimum you could expect between Washington National and Atlanta.

"Fantastic!" he says. "This is amazing! I thank you very much and will talk to you later."

About two weeks after that, I happened to meet Bill in flight operations. He says, "Oh, I found out that you didn't save 1,200 pounds at all."

"Oh?"

"I've been doing the same thing day after day, along with all the people who are flying just like the book says to do. And almost every one of them went over the fuel by over 800 pounds. So you really saved 2,000 pounds over average." Boy, that made me happy. But the reality was that the company rejected any attempts to persuade them of my remarkable and mystifying fuel savings plan. I suspect politics were somehow involved.

Once, I was at a meeting between union and management. I was the safety chairman serving on the local executive council of the union. During negotiations, somebody spoke up. "You should listen to John Billings and save money instead of trying to take it out of our pockets."

The leader from management said, "I remember that exchange. When I was in college," he continued, emphasizing the word *college,* "the amount of thrust to equal the weight of the aircraft needed to be increased in order to go up." It was clear he was thinking of the DC-9 as a rocket ship, which it wasn't.

Finally, I gave up on trying to convince others of my achievement and just kept flying on serendipity. No matter that my trips were saving the company $8,000 a month. They didn't pay me that much. But because I used the system for nearly seven years up until retirement, I was essentially making about $85,000 per year. In a sense, they had me for free.

Chapter 15

Private Wings

Not one to let the ground grow under my feet, in 1975 I started renting airplanes for personal pleasure. I was also instructing on the side, and occasionally one of my students would trade a flying lesson for a trip in his airplane. One time I borrowed a Cessna 170, owned by a student named Frank who'd learned to fly in a little Cessna 140, which he upgraded to the four-seat tail-dragger. "Any time you want to go, take it out and fly," he'd offered.

As we were going to bed one night, I came up with a brilliant idea. "Nancy," I said, "how about we go out and take off before dawn in the Cessna? I have a surprise for you." She agreed, and we rose in the chilly predawn and drove to Manassas where Frank kept his plane. Now there's nothing so beautiful as a sunrise seen from the cockpit. The colors are magnificent – red, magenta, and all shades of orange. The more you look away from the horizon toward the apex, the darker the blue gets, a rich indigo. I told Nancy my gift to her was going to be an unforgettable sunrise. Well, the sun came up as the sun does, but that was all. Just a bright light suddenly filling the sky.

She turned and looked at me. "Is that it?"

"Naturally," I said, "and all because I wanted to show you such great beauty. Do you want to keep flying or go home?"

"We might as well keep going," she said. She wanted to keep going north, and that's what we did, stopping in Williamsport, Pennsylvania, for breakfast, then continuing on to the Finger Lakes region of upstate New York, east around Lake Ontario (wanting to avoid the Canadian side, though in those days, all you needed was a driver's license) to the Thousand Island area and St. Lawrence river with Canada on the opposite bank. In the back of my mind I was concerned about fuel and the fact that the Cessna 170 was an old airplane with an engine that runs best on 80-octane gasoline. With so few airplanes that use it, I thought I'd better find a place soon that provided the fuel we needed.

After making several calls, I finally found an airport in Oneonta, New York, that had the 80 octane. I landed on a grass field with no runway but was able to get fuel, coffee, and lunch. The folks there were looking for conversation and it was hard to get away, but by now it was mid-afternoon and I said we had to get back home. We turned around and headed back, drifting east of the route we'd flown northbound and passing over Philadelphia before turning southwest toward Manassas. It was after dark when we landed. We'd been in the air for eight-and-a-half hours.

Frank was sitting outside where he kept his plane tied down and greeted us. "Where'd you go," he asked.

"Canada."

"Great!" he said. He was proud of that little airplane.

After leaving Eastern in 1983, I rented airplanes so Nancy and I could continue our pleasure trips, but we didn't think highly of the maintenance on the rentals and some of them were pretty uncomfortable. I'd known about a local consortium of five young men who'd bought a new Cessna 172RG so they could learn to fly. Two of them had less than 100 hours of flying time. It so happened that one of the five was a soldier based at Ft. Belvoir, Virginia, who was transferred to San Diego and had to sell his share. He was asking $2,500, which Nancy and I could easily manage at that time, so in March 1987, I became one of the owners of N9649B, or *49 Bravo*, which we kept in Manassas.

At one point, through a close inspection of the books I found out that the group's treasurer was tampering with funds from our flying consortium, and that at least $25,000 was missing! He was an accountant with a business in Rosslyn, Virginia, across the Potomac river from Georgetown, and his office occupied the entire floor of one of the high rises. When we confronted him, he said, "I'd planned to pay it back before anyone noticed." He pleaded with us not to call the sheriff and offered to pay it back at a rate of $1,000 per month, promising that if he missed a payment, he'd increase it by five percent. He paid us for a couple of months, then disappeared. The other club members said that since I was the one who discovered the theft, I was going to be the new treasurer. It happened that two of the young men in the club worked for the World Bank and through connections, that's how they tracked the thief down to Rio de Janiero where he was teaching English to an adult class at night. We figured he'd been dipping into other treasuries, too, but there was nothing we could do about it.

Something else I didn't like was that our airplane had been mortgaged with high interest. So, I bought the mortgage, and instead of paying the bank, the other owners paid me. I charged only three percent instead of the bank's fourteen percent. But sometimes not even favorable financial terms can affect the winds of change.

One day, a fellow owner decided to fly his wife to Boston for a pleasure trip. Everything had gone well until they were heading back home and ran into a squall line in New York. The pilot landed immediately, and it so happened there was no one on the field that he'd chosen, so he just taxied to a place where there were ropes and, with heavy rain battering him, tied the plane down. He got back in and told his wife they wouldn't get wet and would ride out the storm in the airplane. Rain and wind shook the plane ferociously, and after the storm passed, his wife told him in no uncertain terms that she'd never get in that airplane again. That brought our membership down to four of us: the president of the club, the two novices, and me. Well, one day the president announced he was getting a divorce and decided to get rid of the airplane so his wife wouldn't get it. She agreed to sell.

"This isn't a good time to sell an airplane," I told them. "Find a buyer and get the best price you can."

The price they came back with was $24,000. "Are you willing to end up with no airplane and only $4,000?" I asked them. With closing costs estimated to be around $8,000, the figure I quoted was what they would end up with. They agreed to the price, and I bought the plane for $12,000. But I also took over the mortgage, which was nearly $100,000 (and which I still have). If I were to sell *49 Bravo*, it would be worth only a fourth of the mortgage. There was nothing I could do about it. I'd have to eat it.

As a subscriber to the Retired Eastern Pilots Association magazine, I read about pilots who met every month in various cities throughout the country. "Too bad somebody didn't think of meeting in the Washington, D.C., area," I thought. Then it dawned on me that *I'm* somebody, and I got to work organizing a D.C. branch. I was one of the few people who had a computer that could print things, so I took a list of people with their mailing addresses and sent out postcards. We met monthly at a restaurant in Springfield, Virginia. Because some of us had our own planes or had access to them, we decided it would be fun to fly someplace for lunch each month. We called ourselves the Washington Lunch Bunch, and people had a chance to vote on where they wanted to go the next time.

A favorite place was Tangier island, Virginia, that had the best crab cakes and seafood anywhere, not to mention the fascinating history and people of the place separated from the rest of the world by the Chesapeake Bay except by flight or ferry. We went to Summit, Delaware; Hagerstown and Ocean City, Maryland; Williamsburg, Virginia; and Lexington, Kentucky. One of our favorite restaurants occupied the entire upper floor of the Arnold Palmer Regional Airport in southwestern Pennsylvania. Those adventures lasted until the demise of Eastern in 1991. Many of the pilots had gotten bit by the dealings with the new president and got very little of their retirement, which meant they ended up having to sell their airplanes.

It wouldn't be until 2005 that I came to understand *49 Bravo*'s true purpose and my next career as an Angel Flight volunteer pilot. But first, there were a few dangerous storms to be weathered.

Chapter 16

Crosswinds

After I retired, Nancy and I indulged our adventurous spirits and took quite a few cruises. We went to unforgettable places like the South Pacific, Norway, and Russia. While we loved sampling exotic cultures and experiences, we were always glad to get back home. But one homecoming from a short Caribbean cruise in August of 1995 was a return to disaster. Our daughter, Leslie, met us in Alexandria where our ship had docked on the Potomac river. She drove us home to Mt. Vernon and said, "Just leave your bags in the entryway and follow me." We went to the family room where the TV was. In the VCR was a videotape with a big note that said, "Play this." So, we sat down and started the tape, which happened to be *Raiders of the Lost Ark*. The thunderous sounds of shoot-ups and cave-ins were even more thunderous because our kids had bought us a super sound system connected to the television.

"Man, those speakers are something!" I said to Nancy. "I could feel that last boom!"

"Wait a minute," Leslie said, jumping up. "That wasn't in the movie!" She went to the kitchen yelling, "I smell smoke."

"I do too!" It was a strong electrical smell, but I couldn't find the source. Then I went to the door leading to the cellar and opened it. Instantly, I was enveloped in flames, which thank God didn't catch but only singed my hair. I slammed the door. "Get out of the house!" I shouted. Nancy and Leslie rushed out to the patio, and I ran into the living room to grab the phone. It was dead, of course – the wires were all in the basement. The central hall was now a massive torch. I decided to jump through the window Hollywood style to the carport, but instantly remembered that Hollywood glass is make-believe. So, I ran through the dining room, which by now was on fire, to the family room where we'd just been, and then to the outside, where I could see a flame licking its way out of one of the small, sub-level cellar windows. The garden hose was right there, and I pulled on it, but it was so hot, the end came off in my hand. I thought, "I'd better get out of here," and went around to the front looking for Nancy and Leslie. That's when I spotted my other garden hose near the carport. I grabbed it, turned it on, and started pouring water into the flaming cellar window as the vinyl siding melted before my eyes all the way up to the roof.

All of a sudden Leslie appeared and knocked the hose out of my hand. "The house is gonna explode!" she hollered, dragging me away from the site. Back then I did a lot of shooting as a hobby and made my own ammo. Canisters of gunpowder and loaded rounds were stored in the cellar. Fortunately, nothing exploded. Meanwhile, the neighbor had called the fire department. Soon, a fire engine came barreling down our short street with sirens blaring.

"Do you have a key?" the fireman asked me as he strode to the front door. It was locked.

"Yeah, but it's hanging on the kitchen wall."

"That's okay, we'll handle it." His men approached with a big ram and knocked the door flat. When they came out, the fireman asked me what I'd done, and I explained everything.

"Well, you put the fire out," he said.

The day after the fire my mother died. My brother, Bruce, called to deliver the painful news. It was all the more upsetting because I knew I couldn't help with funeral arrangements or even attend her service. "There's no way I can come," I told him. "You're going to have to be the leader of the family right now because I can't get up there."

He was in high distress at the thought of having to manage everything by himself. Our sister, Barbara, was living in Hilton Head, South Carolina, and unable to assist.

It was not a good year. The house was condemned. Nancy and I went to a motel the day of the fire and stayed for three days. After that, we stayed in a "luxury" 700-square-foot apartment for six months. Damages were estimated to be $400,000. We ended up paying $45,000 for what insurance didn't pay. The renovation took six months and included new floor joists, siding, and other repairs, leaving not the slightest trace of smoke.

Finally, we were able to return home the next April. We decided that after our many hardships we should reward ourselves with a cruise, and so we booked a three-week trip from Miami to San Francisco, unsuspecting of the storm that lay ahead. During our years of marriage, we'd taken many cruises and while aboard, we kept in shape by walking up and down the decks instead of using elevators. On this particular trip, Nancy had to stop halfway up the stairs and hang on to the railing to catch her breath. She was a former smoker who'd quit about six years prior, but she had never experienced such difficulty breathing. Despite her dislike of doctors, I put my foot down and said, "When we return, you're going to see the doctor. This isn't right." For the rest of the cruise, a cloud hung over us as she struggled to walk even a few steps.

We returned home to Mt. Vernon in mid-September 1995. Nancy went to a pulmonologist for a consult, then had an endoscopy in vivid color that she and I watched on video. "Here's what we're looking at," said the doctor, showing us pictures fixed from the video. "That's a tumor you're seeing there in the junction of the bronchi. The good one, you could pass a quarter on edge through it. The bad one, you could hardly put a pencil lead through the middle."

It was ugly, scary ugly. Nancy sat there expressionless as the doctor continued. "This is why you're short of breath. You really have only one lung and the other one is at a point where it's dragging down the good one. So, it's a negative asset. Unfortunately, where it lies, it's inoperable." Her face remained impassive. My heart sank.

He went on to give her several options, recommending radiation and chemo. "Radiation would shrink the mass. Chemo would shrink it some more." Nancy had friends who'd gone through chemotherapy, and she would have none of it.

"I'll take the radiation," she said. "Forget chemo. What's that going to do for me?"

"It will extend your life a little and help you to breathe easier."

"What's a little?" she asked.

"Maybe a month or two. We need to put you on a very good physical rehabilitation course." (Nancy wasn't very active.) "And the radiation," he added.

She didn't look at me, not once. She didn't even ask. I wasn't part of it.

She had three radiation treatments. One day, after a friend left from a visit, Nancy said, "Something's wrong. I can't put any weight on this leg."

"Is it painful?" I asked.

"No, no. I mean, I can't put weight on it or I'll fall down." At this point she was holding on to the kitchen counter.

I grabbed the phone and called the radiologist and described what was going on. "Did radiation have anything to do with this?

"Absolutely not," he answered. "It's something else. You should take her to the emergency room right now."

I hung up and said, "Come on, Nancy." It was a chore for her to walk the twenty-five feet to the front door with me supporting her. When we got outside the door to go to the car, she collapsed on me. As I struggled to get her up, my neighbor drove up, and I yelled for his attention. The two of us managed to get her in the car, and I sped to the hospital in Mt. Vernon, which fortunately was only five miles away. It didn't have a typical emergency room that you could drive right up to. Instead, the ER was by the front door. I parked on the sidewalk and ran inside. "I need a wheelchair!" I yelled.

The room was full of people, and the clerk signing in patients pointed across the room and said, "There's some wheelchairs over there." I grabbed one, went out, and with much effort, got my wife into the wheelchair and rolled her in. With a long line in front of us, it was a good solid hour before we got to the desk to explain what was wrong. It seems there had been a gun fight and knife fight. People were bleeding all over the place, and of course they were being taken care of. By comparison, there seemed to be nothing wrong with Nancy, sitting quietly in the wheelchair. By now it was 3:30 in the afternoon.

Finally, an orderly came out and said, "We're taking her back and will call you when we have more information." I kissed her goodbye and told her I'd be in the waiting room. The big automatic doors opened and he rolled her through. I went back to my seat. No call came. About 6:30 that evening, Leslie went by the house and seeing no one, figured something bad had happened. She called the hospital and, with the news that her mother was there, came over and joined me in the waiting room.

"How is she? Do they know what's wrong?" she asked.

"They'll let us know," I said.

At 9:00, the orderly showed up and said, "Come on back. We're admitting her."

"For what?" I asked.

"I don't know. First thing they're going to do is sedate her so she'll go right to sleep. Come back in the morning." Later, I learned that Nancy had lain on a gurney in a hallway for about six hours.

We went home to a restless night, and when we returned to the hospital in the morning, we were directed to her room. A nurse was in the small bathroom preparing something.

"Nancy, how are you feeling?" I leaned over to stroke her forehead and she answered me with unintelligible babbling as if she'd been drinking and was stoned to the gills. I couldn't recognize a word coming out of her mouth. I went to the nurse. "What are they doing to her? Have they thought of anything?"

"I'm not sure," she replied. "I'm preparing a sedative right now."

"You're giving her another sedative? Why, she's totally incoherent now! No one here has done a thing for her!" I was beside myself. As it turns out, they were going to give her an MRI, but because she was so agitated and unable to calm down, they couldn't do the test.

Not long after, the doctor came in to talk to us. "In my opinion, she's had a stroke," he said. It had taken him a day to figure it out. At the time I didn't know what I know now, that the first ninety minutes are the only window of time available to prevent the devastating effects of stroke. Less than a month later, she would be gone.

The weeks leading up to Nancy's death were weeks of painful struggle. She had to continue her radiation treatments, but these were in a different hospital and she had to travel back and forth. As it was taking quite a toll on her, the doctor decided to admit her to that hospital. It was the beginning of the end. She contracted staph. I first knew about it when I went to visit her as I did every day and was greeted by a sign in red letters covering her door: Isolation. I had to wear a gown and mask. So did Leslie, who came often to help, and any other visitors. At this point, Nancy couldn't speak at all and tried to scribble her messages. But her handwriting had deteriorated so much, I couldn't read a word. I can imagine how frustrating it was for her, and then not to be able to see our faces because of the masks we had to wear.

"We've done as much as we can." I don't remember the date when the doctor came in to deliver those dreaded words. Time was a blur. "I recommend you contact a hospice," he said matter-of-factly. I called the number the hospital had provided, and it was like lighting a firecracker, so quick were they to get things rolling. "First you need to get everything out of the room that you want to keep."

Leslie and I took down all the get-well cards that I'd stuck on the wall where Nancy could see them, and then we got all the flowers we could. By the time we arrived home, hospice was already there. They'd set up a hospital bed in the family room, then other medical providers arrived with an oxygen machine since Nancy was on 100 percent oxygen. They brought other equipment, too, and all the things needed for our home hospital. An attending nurse was there who would come every other day to provide comfort, like bathing and making sure the bed was adjusted properly. She installed a port so morphine could be injected for pain. Every hour around the clock I had to give Nancy morphine. I pulled an air mattress out of the attic and kept an alarm clock beside me so I could sleep between syringes. She had to be fed through a stomach tube, and I was in charge of that operation as well. Susan and Lee came to see their mom when they could, but distance made those trips difficult.

Six days after coming home, she died. It was November 25, 1995, and I was with her. All of a sudden, she struggled for a big breath of air and that was it. Later, the nurse told me that the gasping which had disturbed me so profoundly was the body's reaction to the end. Nancy and I had made advance arrangements with the funeral home. Neither of us believed in burial, so the funeral people came promptly and courteously, and took the body away. Several days later a little box of ashes arrived. Nancy had told me long before any of this happened that she wanted her ashes to be sprinkled in our pet cemetery behind the house, which was a wooded area. And that's what Leslie and I did on a cold autumn day.

Chapter 17

Barbara

I first met Barbara Barrett in 1959 on a trip to Savannah, Georgia. I was in New York then and working for Eastern. It was a meeting that would change my life, only I didn't know it the instant she stepped into the cockpit and introduced herself in a voice like a song. "Hello, my name is Barbara Barrett, and I'm the flight attendant on this trip." I turned around, and our eyes locked. All I could see were her pupils. It was electrifying.

I was flying a Martin 404 from LaGuardia field to Columbia, South Carolina, for the first leg and Savannah, Georgia, for the second. In fact, I would be spending two nights in Savannah because we'd be arriving at 9:00 that night, and the trip out of Savannah was at 7 a.m., too small an overnight by regulation. The airplane could carry only forty passengers, so just one flight attendant was required, and she was Barbara Barrett. During the flight, I don't think I've ever had so many cups of coffee offered to me! I didn't get a good look at her until we got to Savannah. I was speechless. All I could do was stare at her, making a fool of myself over this woman with dark blond hair, a big smile, and eyes I fell into. She was a real beauty. After we arrived and the three of us settled into our rooms at the historic Desoto Hotel, we all went out for a late supper. We swapped stories about our adventures in flight, and Barbara asked me about my military career.

After dinner, we went back to our rooms and changed into swimsuits for a dip in the pool. As I climbed out a few laps later, I announced that I was turning in for the night as my co-pilot had already done. "It's been a long day," I said.

"Say, I've got an idea." Barbara was smiling mischievously. "Let's change our clothes and go walking in the parks. We can stay up all night!"

In Savannah, you can't go a single block without finding yourself in a park under arching live oaks dripping with Spanish moss. It was a warm night full of moonlight and happy conversation. We walked for miles, and there seemed to be no time. So, we were surprised to hear a carillon from a nearby church saluting the day. I thanked her for the pleasure of her company and she thanked me for mine.

During the month, we flew two more times on that same trip. Without saying it, we knew we were in love and couldn't deny the powerful current passing back and forth. Back home in New York, I went to my darkroom, where having the door shut meant "do not open," since opening it might expose and ruin the film I might be developing. I needed the darkness and privacy. I needed to develop my thoughts, for I was engaged in a formidable battle with myself, pulled by the choice to leave my family, pulled back to stay. So it went for hours. For good or bad, I don't know, but I decided that leaving wasn't what a man should do. I never told anyone, not even Barbara.

Meanwhile, Barbara was also thinking about us and decided we were getting in too deep. Because she didn't want to be a family disrupter and, without saying a word to me, she put in a bid for Atlanta. After the fact, she told me in a letter that she had transferred to Atlanta. Through the years we occasionally passed each other at the airport. Those encounters were always stiff and impersonal. "Oh, I hear that the seating capacity has risen," or, "Captain So and So's retiring next month" – that sort of small talk. Anything we felt for each other was kept in strict abeyance, though I admit, she lived in my dreams for years – vivid dreams where we shared adventures together.

Years later, Barbara called to ask if I could help her with her computer. She liked to write short stories and had learned I was pretty good at messing around with computers, which were still in the early stages of development. I agreed and went several times to her house to make suggestions and explain how this or that was done. Her husband was home, of course.

Thirty-seven years after our first meeting, the phone rang and it was Barbara. She'd heard about Nancy's death and wanted to offer her condolences. Not surprisingly, we seemed to have a lot to talk about. I'm not sure who brought it up, but we finally decided to meet for lunch and catch up on the last forty years of our lives. It was then that she told me she was in the midst of a divorce. Having thought for all those years that hers was a perfect marriage and a perfect life, I was stunned. I could hardly speak. After a moment or so, I got my wits together and remembered I had an appointment scheduled with the attorney handling Nancy's probate. His office wasn't far from Annandale, Virginia, where Barbara worked as the receptionist for a dentist. I told her I'd be free around one o'clock and we agreed on a place to meet.

It was in a hotel restaurant over a three-hour lunch that she told me the litigation for her divorce was advancing slowly. She'd left her career with the airlines when she married because back in the Sixties, a flight attendant couldn't be married. There was so much to talk about! Our families and careers, our mutual and unspoken decision not to pursue the relationship, the love we shared for each other that had remained locked inside through the years . . . until that momentous afternoon.

At the end of our time together that day, I asked Barbara if she would ever marry again. The answer was a resounding "No!" She asked me the same question, and I answered as she had, and likewise emphatically. We both left that day happy to reconnect as old friends and happy that there were no strings attached. And yet, we were a bit excited about the possibilities of enjoying a safe friendship and sharing an occasional lunch or dinner.

I did call Barbara in March and left a message inviting her to go flying in my little airplane. She declined. But she then invited me to go with her on a house-hunting adventure to the Shenandoah Valley, as she was in the process of selling her home and planned to move to the Valley. She said she was looking for an older house and thought that I would be a good resource for checking out heating, plumbing, electrical, and other things about an old house that she in her enthusiasm might miss. Well, I've always loved the Shenandoah Valley and the thought of being with Barbara I loved even better!

We left before daylight on the day of our excursion and continued catching up with each other over breakfast in a Front Royal diner. We traveled through beautiful Fort Valley and reached Woodstock in good time for her appointment with the realtor. It's interesting to me now that the first property the realtor showed us was a handsome, very stately, almost 100-year-old house that felt just wonderful to me: a two-story, four-over-four house on almost an acre right in town with an incredible vista. Now who was showing enthusiasm? Anyway, while she liked the house, Barbara realized that it was much too big for her to manage on her own and quickly checked it off the list. We spent the rest of the day looking at many interesting homes, but none were just right for her. We ended the day at the old Spring House Restaurant in town for a long, leisurely dinner, then took a walk around town. Afterwards, we headed back to Northern Virginia where I delivered my lovely friend and future wife to her house.

Seven months after our luncheon reunion, Barbara bought that stately house in Woodstock, where we now live. Her divorce became final in

September of 1997, and we became engaged almost immediately, setting the wedding date for the coming Thanksgiving.

Our wedding was decidedly unconventional. We agreed we didn't want a fancy church wedding. "So, how about doing something on the spur of the moment?" I suggested.

We came up with a plan to host Thanksgiving dinner at our house and spring the nuptials on our unsuspecting guests. We sent out 100 invitations. Barbara's brother, Richard, and his wife, who lived in Florida, told us they weren't coming, so she had to let out the secret. "You've got to come, and you can't tell a soul!" she warned. Naturally, we told the minister from Barbara's church who would be officiating.

The weeks passed swiftly and Thanksgiving was almost upon us, and for it, Barbara and I did most of the catering. I baked the ham the night before. She had to work and didn't get to Woodstock until about 6:30 that night. We continued our Thanksgiving preparations and went to bed exhausted and excited. Early in the morning we were awakened by a fierce windstorm that rattled the tin roof mightily and blew down branches. So much for the outdoor wedding we'd planned. "Oh, no! How are we going to fit everyone inside?" was our mutual thought. Seventy-eight people had RSVP'd they were coming! Barbara sent me to the attic for extra tablecloths, and as I fished through one of the large trunks, I noticed how quiet things had become. "John, come down here!" she yelled. We went outside to perfect calm and hugged each other in the beautiful sunshine of eight o'clock, certain it was a sign from above. We then put the turkey and the standing rib roast in the oven.

One of our earliest guests was Fred Mayer, from OSS days. He and I had reconnected in 1965 after discovering we lived only 100 miles away from each other. He arrived in a suit and tie with a gift in hand. I said to him, "Fred, I had announced that it was to be casual dress."

He says, "I know what I'm doing. Here, don't open it," and thrust the box to me. "I'll tell you when." Later, when he gave the okay, we unwrapped a beautiful fourteen-inch Lennox wedding platter. Fred was smarter than anyone I'd ever known – he'd figured out the *real* meaning behind his invitation, which merely stated that we had an announcement to make at noon.

Once all the guests were gathered in the backyard, Barbara stepped forward on the deck. "As you all know, we told you we were going to have an announcement at 12:00. We have decided on a date," she said. "Lori," and she turned to her youngest daughter, "I'd like you to be my maid of honor."

Then she proceeded to call all of her closest friends, none younger than fifty, to come on up to be her "bridesmaids." All her friends were excited. "Pick me!" they shouted and came rushing up to the deck. By the end they had all figured out what was going to happen next.

Then I spoke up. "I want Fred Mayer and Dick Gottleber to be my best men because of everybody living now, he and Dick from my crew are the oldest people I know." Dick had come all the way from Michigan with his wife, Lenore. Behind the scenes, Barbara and I had worked up a little script with the minister, now beside us, and were ready to enact it. It was getting to be very crowded on our rickety deck.

"Reverend," I said, "would you be willing to marry us?"

"Well, it depends on what date you choose."

"How about November 27, 1997?"

"Why, that's today!" he exclaimed. "You mean you want to marry this woman *today?*"

"Yes, that's right," I said.

Then he turned to Barbara. "You mean you want to marry *this* man today?"

And she said, "Yes, that's right." With that, he put his hand in his pocket, pulled out a clerical collar, and slipped it in place. Then we overheard Lori whisper, "Oh, they're going to do it right now! If I had known, I would have dressed better."

And so we were happily joined as husband and wife before an astounded and absolutely delighted audience. And this is when we lost control because I said, "Is anybody hungry?" With that the mob made a dash for the kitchen, which was what you might call compact. At one point the minister said, "Are you going to say grace?" and I said, "I don't think so. We've lost it!"

Finally, on Sunday, we left for the Poconos and our honeymoon. We'd had to delay the trip for a couple of days because of weather and because we still had a houseful of company with all beds filled, and an inflated mattress and sleeping bags on the floor. Once we arrived at the resort, which was a favorite destination for newlyweds, we breathed in the fresh mountain air and couldn't stop smiling at each other. A road ran right through the middle of the place with a sign that read, "Caution: Dears Crossing."

Barbara continued working for the dentist, and we kept the Mt. Vernon house. We stayed there through the week and spent weekends in Woodstock. It was the best of both worlds, we thought, having a home in the country and one in the city. As more and more of the dentist's office work shifted to digital files and records, Barbara was able to work from home on the computer in Woodstock and reduce her on-site visits in Annandale.

Gradually, we noticed a change. It would happen when we were nearing Woodstock after driving the two-hour stretch from Mt. Vernon. As we came out westbound and crested the hill, Massanutten Mountain would suddenly rise before us like a beautiful blue wave, and we'd get emotional. "Here we are crossing over – we're in heaven already," we'd say. "We don't have to die." It didn't take us long to sell the Mt. Vernon house and settle into "Our Town." That's what I would always say to Barbara when we were driving on I-81 as we approached Woodstock. I would look at her, smile at our invocation of Thornton Wilder, and say, "Our Town."

Our life together was good. We were active in various cultural, civic, and social activities in our vibrant mountain town. We took road trips and did a lot of flying in *49 Bravo*. We visited Helen Keller's home in Tuscumbia, Alabama, and took a nostalgic flight to Houston for a bomb group reunion, highlighted by the 1940s-themed banquet in the hotel and the company of the Tuskegee Airmen.

In the spring of 2002, after a trip to Italy, Barbara was diagnosed with breast cancer. We were overwhelmingly thankful that it was caught at an early stage. The doctor had cleared her to go on the Italy trip, a kind of sentimental journey for me that was organized by members of the 484th Bomb Group, with four squadrons represented. The idea was to try to find remnants of the old air base at Torretta. We found some buildings, including an old Quonset hut, and couldn't help wondering how the rust was held up! It was disappointing that not the slightest trace of either of the two runways or taxiways remained. But we did see a familiar object propped against the side of someone's house – a piece of pierced steel planking about six feet long and two feet wide that carried us hip-deep in nostalgia. It was part of what was called the Marston Mat, a portable runway made of interlocking planks laid on dirt to hold up the B-24. It's considered one of the greatest inventions of World War II and is still in use today.

Upon our return, Barbara entered the hospital for surgery, and we spent the summer shuffling back and forth to Winchester for her radiation treatments, followed by the discovery of all restaurants between there and Woodstock serving breakfast.

In 2006 we bought a magnificent 21-day Peruvian tour, with adventures ahead that we'd never imagined. We started out in Lima and had various lodgings ranging from a luxurious resort to a primitive tourist camp with a privy and a rope-drawn bucket for a shower. We traveled upriver on the

Amazon, first on a double-deck river boat and then on longboats powered by outboard motors, with visits to a scientific station in the jungle, a monkey preserve, native villages, and other wondrous places.

Other highlights of our trip included hiking to the famed ruins of Machu Picchu and eating roasted potatoes with native Peruvians who built their stoves out of mud. Cleanup was easy. They just destroyed the stove. One day we took a trip on a motorized boat made of reeds tied together. The boat had large ornamental dragon heads as figureheads. We visited the floating islands of Lake Titicaca. These were also made of reeds and were actually little villages of three or four residences inhabited by the Uros tribe. The natives who live there predate the warlike Incas. In ancient days the Uros people would hide in the reeds to survive and at some point, discovered they could make islands of them. Today's inhabitants watch TV at night operated by solar-powered batteries. Technology is unstoppable everywhere!

Unfortunately, our lifetime adventure ended with a mishap. We were staying in a hotel at Lake Titicaca, the largest lake in South America and common to both Bolivia and Peru. At 12,600 feet above sea level from the surface, it's the highest elevation lake in the world with ocean-going vessels. Our room had a view of the vast, dazzling blue lake. Barbara and I shared a single suitcase, one large enough to hold both of our belongings. As I hoisted the heavy suitcase onto the lightweight luggage rack, it started sliding across the tiles with the suitcase half falling off, so I impulsively scrambled to catch it. It ignited an old back injury, and I spent the night soaking in a tub of hot water trying to get relief from the pain.

Rewinding to 1975 when I first hurt my back, I was at the Manassas Airport attempting to lift an airplane out of the mud. The Bonanza was there for overnight only and parked on the grass. During the night it had rained heavily, and the plane sank in the mud. After landing from a flight, a friend and I went to help out the pilot, which turned out to be a bad idea. Instead of getting equipment for the job as we should have done, my friend and I each went under a wing to lift while the pilot pushed the power up, hoping to get the plane out of the mud. Well, it didn't. The only thing that happened was that I ended up face down in the mud and had seriously injured my back. Somehow, I managed to drive home. I had a VW clutch and had to reach down with my hand and pull my leg up to shift from the floor to the pedal. I thought it would be better by morning, but the pain had only increased.

BARBARA

Nancy drove me to the doctor who was the chief of orthopedics at Fairfax Hospital. After days of bed rest, pain meds, and X-rays, he said, "You've got a bulging disc. I can operate on it if you want, but I think the body can do a better job. You just have to be prepared for a very long time for it to heal." I was still working for Eastern Airlines and had stored up enough sick days for the seven months needed for recovery. At first, I took it easy, then the doctor fitted me with a brace, followed by prescribed physical therapy. That entailed my carrying a backpack filled with thirty-five pounds of bricks and a mile of walking with that weight twice a day. But the treatment worked, and seven months later I returned to being a pilot for Eastern.

To return to my story of Peru, Barbara and I had to forego the Bolivian tour scheduled for the day after my injury. We stayed in the hotel and took it easy. Surprisingly, I didn't feel too bad, and we were able to fly home the following day, a seven or so hours' flight to Atlanta. Then we took a bus to Peachtree Airport where *49 Bravo* was waiting to get us safely home.

Life in Woodstock went on pleasantly and productively. I was flying Angel Flight missions, giving talks and interviews about my World War II adventures, making improvements to our house, and doing other worthwhile things. My back hurt somewhat but not enough to trouble me, at least not until it worsened and not until my left leg became numb every now and then, causing me to fall if I wasn't near a chair or counter to hang on to. The situation grew intolerable, and I agreed to surgery. This was in 2008. The operation would take place in Winchester, Virginia, where a leading spinal surgeon would fuse my spine. I agreed, and the surgery was scheduled. The surgical team opened up my back and inserted titanium rods with big screws. Then they took out four of the "doughnuts" – that is, discs – and filled the vacancy with donor bones. It cost me three inches of height. The surgery cured the numbing but not the pain, which came later and for always.

The recovery process was shorter than I'd expected, lasting only about a month. The doctor prescribed oxycodone for pain and gave me a whole pound of it, instructing me to take one or two every four hours for pain. I took one, only one. It destroyed my mind. The rooms of my house looked surreal, and my balance was off when I stood or tried to walk. That was it for me. I would rather have pain than lose my mind. You can stand pain, but if your brain is shot, what good are you? So, I went back to the doctor with all five bottles full of oxycodone and said, "No thank you."

The pain shows up in my lower back. Sometimes, if I stand up quickly, there's a little gremlin in there with a hot spike that pokes me. So, I've

105

learned to baby my back, to do only what I can do. One big problem with getting old is that the body gets old faster than the brain does. The brain can still do things even when the body protests. But aging has its advantages, too. Barbara, for example, decided she didn't really want to fly in my little plane anymore and justified it by saying, "I'm seventy and I don't have to do anything I don't want to do!"

Chapter 18

Hugs and Smiles

Like most people, I'd never heard of Angel Flight. I was aware of public benefit flying; for example, I'd seen magazine ads for Corporate Angel Network, a business group that allowed patients free travel on corporate flights if space was available. Then one day I happened to be in an FBO (Fixed Base Operator, for general aviation) in Latrobe, Pennsylvania, and noticed a display with a question that drew me like a magnet: "Do you want to fly for Angel Flight?"

Angel Flight is a nonprofit organization of volunteer pilots who use their own or rented planes to fly patients to distant medical appointments free of charge. Their slogan is, "The shortest distance between home and hope." I liked that! I decided that helping people in need would be a good use of *49 Bravo*, so I wrote down the phone number for Angel Flight Mid-Atlantic (one of several different regions in the U.S.) and called the headquarters in Virginia Beach, Virginia. The mission coordinator, MaryJane ("MJ") Sablan, gave me the information and requirements for becoming a volunteer pilot. This included such things as having a minimum of 500 hours as Pilot in Command (PIC), a minimum of 50 hours in the airplane that would be used for patient flights, an annual medical checkup, and regulations governing the licensing and condition of the airplane.

Quite a few measures had to be taken before I was ready to fly for Angel Flight – my plane, for starters. I kept my Cessna 172RG in a hangar in Newmarket, Virginia. The hangar was primitive, to say the least, and had four doors that ran on overhead tracks. To get in, I had to push them to the side. The FBO didn't provide extra tracks, so first I had to go to the hangar to my right, push those two doors aside, then to the one on the left, and push those aside. Obviously, no one could lock their hangar. The floor was made of crushed stones. *49 Bravo* was heavy, but I was young enough that I could muscle it out, at least for a while. That got old quick, so I bought a tow bar and hitch that I installed on the front of my Izuzu Trooper. That helped, but maneuvering was difficult because the Trooper was so long, I couldn't make sharp turns. Later on, my good friend Fred Mayer searched and found a small, hydraulically-driven lawnmower tractor that no longer had blades but plenty of power, and I used that.

Another problem was that I couldn't put anything in the hangar because the roof leaked badly, leaving the airplane subject to the elements. Most of the people at Newmarket didn't fly at all in the winter, but I did and had to use the Trooper to force the doors to break the ice. One day my mechanic, who happened to be the mechanic at Newmarket, asked how much I had to pay.

"$169," I told him.

"You pay me the same amount and I'll give you a space in the maintenance hangar," he said. That was huge. That hangar could hold up to five planes at a time. "I'll always rearrange things so you're at the head of the line. That way you can always get your airplane when you need it." In January 2007, I moved the plane to Manassas (HEF) to where my mechanic had relocated, and then in October 2008, I moved it to Luray (now designated LUA) where the plane is still kept. It takes about forty-five minutes to get there from my house in Woodstock.

The Cessna 172RG was as basic as it gets, with no redundancy for anything. In other words, there was only one source for information. So, I grounded the airplane and spent the better part of a year outfitting it with what I wanted to put in it. I have old pictures of the plane all torn apart with wires every which-way. Figuring I'd be flying by myself, I wanted a professional avionics system with fully redundant navigation and communications that were capable of low visibility, instrument (IFR) approaches. After extensive checks to see what *49 Bravo* could do, and with Barbara's encouragement, I joined Angel Flight Mid-Atlantic.

My first mission was in February 2005. I went to Tazewell, Virginia, to pick up the patient, a man in his fifties, and his friend, and flew them to the University of Virginia Medical Center in Charlottesville where the patient was to get a bone marrow transplant. It was a good feeling, knowing someone's life would be improved because of my Angel Flight. The second trip was an eye-opener. I picked up a married couple in Allentown, Pennsylvania. The mission brief said the man was getting dialysis and his wife was getting kidney tests. I thought, "Man, that's pretty bad for both the husband and wife to have kidney problems." They were relatively young. Turns out the wife was deathly afraid of flying. She got in the back seat and literally put her head in her lap. I was quite concerned, but her husband reassured me that it was okay for us to go, that she just didn't like to fly. At one point, we broke through a layer of clouds and the husband said to his wife, "Look, honey, look out the window. The tops of the clouds are beautiful!"

I glanced out of the corner of my eye, saw her lift up her head, look out, and then put her head back into hiding as she muttered, "Yes, it's beautiful."

"It's very unlucky that you both have problems with kidneys," I said. "It usually doesn't happen that way."

"Oh, no," said the man. "My kidney's the one that's no good. She came along to test to see if her kidney's a match for a transplant."

"You mean to say she came up here, scared to death of flying as she is, just to give you a kidney or the possibility of a kidney?"

"Yes, that's it," he answered.

"Well," I said, "you'd better mind your manners and keep her smiling."

This encounter affected me profoundly. Throughout my Angel Flight service, I continually find it amazing that people who have critical conditions and diseases seldom complain. They have beautiful, big smiles on their faces even when technically speaking they're on death's doorstep. That was the case with a little boy named Ethan. When he was only seven months old, he contracted meningitis. His parents made the agonizing decision to save his life by having his arms and legs amputated. I picked up Ethan and Heather, his young mother, and flew them to Lewisburg, West Virginia, to be handed over to another Angel Flight pilot who would be providing the trip to Cincinnati Children's Hospital in Ohio. I held little Ethan while his mother got settled in the back seat. A week short of his first birthday, he weighed only seven and a half pounds – less than my cat.

The infection had destroyed most of his face: he didn't have a nose, and his mouth was a tiny hole. I've flown him several times, as he has to have frequent surgeries. He's now about fourteen years old. His father rigged up a device that allows him to go fishing, and he also outfitted a remotely controlled, battery-powered toy car that his son could operate. Ethan is happy as a clam. That's what I mean about the patients I take on Angel Flights. We complain about a little backache, but they have an astounding ability to live joyful lives.

Joyful is the word to describe my frequent fliers, Leanne and Cristina Powell. Leanne is treated by a leading specialist in pain management at Brigham Women's Medical Center in Boston. She was injured in a terrible car accident years ago and relies on Angel Flight to convey her and Cristina, her daughter and caregiver, back and forth from their home in Michigan. Cristina was adopted from Peru when she was only four days old. Then, at fifteen months, she was diagnosed with cerebral palsy and a movement disorder. She wasn't expected to be able to walk or talk, but not only does she walk and talk, she's an accomplished artist who, with her mom, received a standing ovation when she and her mom did a TED Talk in Boston on January 25, 2018. You can watch it on YouTube. Cristina has her own nonprofit called A Brighter Way and gives away her cheerful, colorful paintings to cancer patients and others suffering from serious medical conditions. These two ladies are joined at the hip. Like the other patients I fly for Angel Flight, they reward me with hugs and smiles.

One of my Angel Flight passengers is world famous. Richard Norris was headlined all over the planet in 2012 for having the most comprehensive face transplant up until that time. Fifteen years before that, a gun accident left him without lips, a nose, teeth, and part of his tongue. He lived behind a mask in his Hillsville, Virginia, home and stayed away from public places, shopping at night for groceries. I was the first pilot to take him to the University of Maryland Medical Center in Baltimore in 2005 when he began a series of facial surgeries, but none could really restore him – not until a young man's death made it possible for Richard to have a face.

The operation, led by Dr. Eduardo Rodriguez at Maryland Shock and Trauma Center, took two days and involved more than 150 medical people. Richard got a new jaw, teeth, tongue, and skin from scalp to neck. As time went on, the anti-rejection drugs began to take a toll on Richard's kidneys and he ended up on dialysis and in desperate need of a kidney. Once again, Providence was on his side and in June 2019, he underwent transplant surgery. The donor was his nephew.

A stroke of great luck in my own life is a man named Nevin Showman. He's my Angel Flight partner, co-pilot, and closest friend. It was through Barbara that we met in 2009. Nevin owned a TV and electronics store, Edinburg Electronics Sales and Service, in a town next door to Woodstock. At the time, the building was divided into two shops, half of it Nevin's and the other half, his wife Sharon's. She had a curio shop and sold gifts and decorative items. One day Barbara decided to stop by Nevin's shop to check about a TV. She spotted a series of airplane pictures on the wall of his display room and stopped to study the small planes.

"May I help you?" he offered.

"Are you a pilot?" she asked.

"Well, sort of."

This led to a lively conversation about flying and airplanes. When Barbara got home, she said, "John, you've got to go to Edinburg and meet a man named Nevin." As it happened, our television set was acting up and the images were different shades of red. I gave Nevin a call and described the problem.

"Yes, I'm familiar with that model," he said, and agreed to make a house call.

He came over and explained why repairing our existing set, an older-model, rear-projection TV, would be costly and that he could sell us a new TV for a lot less money, one that would fit into the cabinet that we wanted to keep. Nevin came back a few days later with a new wide-screen television, and the conversation turned to airplanes and Angel Flight. I learned that he'd gotten his private pilot's license in 1998 and for a time he flew around in search of the proverbial hundred-dollar hamburger. But then he stopped flying altogether because of the expense. I told him about Angel Flight and the cancer patients and others who could get access to life-saving treatment because of the free flights we provided.

"Just a little while ago, Angel Flight came out with a new rule," I said to Nevin. "A pilot over seventy-five should do his best to have a co-pilot with him on every trip." Of course, I was past seventy and had done my first Angel Flight at age seventy-four. I asked Nevin if he'd like to be my co-pilot.

"That would be fine," Nevin said. "I'd like to fly with you." I explained that I had email addresses for all the pilots who had shown interest in accompanying me on Angel Flights, so when a request came up, I would send out notices to those pilots. Whoever responded first would fly right seat.

As soon as the next mission became available, I sent out my email requests. Nevin was the first to sign up, so he got to be my co-pilot. The flight was on December 4, 2009, from Raleigh-Durham to Frederick, Maryland. Our passenger, Char, was a frequent flyer with Angel Flight and a brave cancer warrior. Nevin really liked that experience and was quick to be first for the next several missions. But suddenly I stopped getting emails from him.

"Your business certainly is booming," I told him the next time we spoke.

"What do you mean?" he asked.

"I figure you've gotten pretty busy. All of a sudden it's other people signing up to fly with me."

"Well, I thought about it, Captain, and realized I'm taking the position away from a lot of others who might like to do it. I wanted to be fair, so I just haven't been signing up."

"This is quite a dilemma," I thought to myself. "I know just how to solve it." And so I did. I stopped posting emails and just called Nevin.

He's a fantastic man, one of the kindest, most congenial individuals I've ever known. Nevin has a unique family life. He and Sharon take care of his sister Patty, who at fifty-five is a year younger than Nevin. Only her mind is probably four years old. Everything has to be done for her. Most people wouldn't tolerate a situation like that but would throw up their hands and say, "Oh, she must be institutionalized." Of course, patients like that don't live very long in institutions. Nevin had promised his parents that Patty would have a home with him for as long as he lived. It used to be that when I dropped by the house, Patty wouldn't even look at me. Gradually, as she started recognizing me, her greeting was "Man." Now it's "John."

This is a remarkable family that serves one another. A number of years ago a trailer was set up on Nevin's property. His parents lived there until they passed away. Now his sister, Bonnie, lives there. For a long time she would take over the care of Patty to give Sharon and Nevin time away to be together. Now Mikayla, a grand-niece living under Nevin and Sharon's custody, has been added to that family permanently. He and Sharon are raising what amounts to a seven-year-old daughter who in turn completely adores them and calls them Mom and Dad. Bonnie, happily, steps up whenever help is needed. That's their system of how a family operates. They all have oars in the water propelling the boat forward.

When I first knew him, Nevin was a neophyte pilot. He'd never flown in a complex airplane, just a basic Cessna and Piper. Licensed to fly in 1998, he had memorized everything the instructor told him, but his training didn't progress beyond that. One day I said, "Let's go up in the airplane and you'll fly it. We'll go down to Shenandoah and do some landings and take-offs." As if working from a script, he took off ritually, flew down, and made a ritual landing. The normal pattern would extend considerably beyond the end of the runway: turn ninety degrees toward it, another ninety degrees toward it, then fly back straight in and land. So, I had Nevin fly down, land, take off, make a pattern, land – I did that four times without saying anything more.

Then the fifth time, about halfway downwind (which is opposite to the direction of landing but parallel to the runway), I reached over and closed the throttle, saying, "You've just had an engine failure. You've tried everything and it won't start again. Now continue." Nevin looked around, made a close-in circular pattern, and landed. I mean, it was a beautiful landing. "Any comments?" I asked him.

"That felt good!" was all he said.

"Okay, let's take the airplane back to Luray and go back home."

As we continued flying together, he paid close attention to my way of doing things. I warned him that if he kept doing that, he'd pick up my bad habits. The worst one is that I don't follow the script. As I've explained to Nevin and other novice pilots, the most valuable device in the cockpit of any airplane is found inside the pilot's head. Because not every situation a pilot might be confronted with has been documented, the ability to think is the most important asset; in such cases, there is no script. I've often wondered why my airplane hasn't been grounded, because many times when it was Nevin's turn to fly the last leg of a trip going back to Luray, the engine would strangely quit. (Actually, I was the culprit.) My purpose was for him to recognize the fact that he couldn't make it to the field and that he'd have to figure out what to do. "I've got to put it in that grass field over there," is one of those things he figured out without a script.

Now Nevin can do anything I can. I encouraged him to get his instrument rating to qualify for Angel Flight, which he did. "But you're not qualified until you make your first patient trip as pilot in command (PIC)," I said. He asked me which mission I wanted him to do. "I don't know, 'cause I'm not going with you!" I answered. So, Nevin took his first solo Angel Flight, picked up his patient, and landed in Pittsburgh. By 2009 he'd accumulated far more than the minimum 500 hours required as PIC, and he became an official Angel Flight pilot.

To give you an idea of why he's a great co-pilot, I relate a story told to me when I first sat in the right seat. When you see two pilots walking into operations from the ramp or going out of operations to the ramp, you can tell which is which without a uniform because the one doing all the work is the co-pilot, but the one taking all the credit is the captain.

Chapter 19

Wings Around America

One day, sometime in mid-2015, Nevin and I were on our way home from an Angel Flight when he said, "Hey, have you ever thought of taking the airplane out and just looking at the Pacific Ocean, then coming back?"

I looked at him. "You know, I've had a bucket list item for years and years. I've always wanted to take off and fly the periphery of the country."

Nevin grinned. "Okay, I'll take care of the ground costs. You take care of the airplane costs."

That was the beginning of Wings Around America. Our purpose was bigger than a wish on my bucket list. We undertook it with the serious goal of raising awareness of public benefit flying and of Angel Flight in particular. Good ole *49 Bravo* was decked out with a couple of Angel Flight patches and a sign for Holtzman Oil Corp. We needed funds for the flight, and Bill Holtzman wrote us a personal check for a hefty amount. We also had thirty boxes of American flags made here in the U.S. and including signed (by us) and dated certificates to be given to people who donated $250 to BWC, the company that owns the airplane.

Our adventure began at 9:00 a.m. on July 26, 2015, at Luray Caverns Airport. A TV reporter from a Harrisonburg, Virginia, station was on hand to cover the story. A small group of friends and supporters were there for the send-off as well. Nevin and I had laid out parameters in advance, allocating an entire month for the trip. We agreed to fly only on days that would allow for good photography, as we wanted to do a photo and video journal. This can be seen on the website Nevin created during the trip so our followers could be "virtual" passengers day by day along our route: www.WingsAroundAmerica.com. We planned on two stops a day, weather permitting, but the trip ended up being a total of thirteen flying days.

The first day of our journey gave us stunning aerial views of Thomas Jefferson's getaway home, Poplar Forest, in Virginia; large, open pits of defunct copper mines in Copperhill, Tennessee; the Edmund Pettus Bridge in Selma, Alabama, where Martin Luther King famously marched; and finally, New Orleans and Lake Pontchartrain.

Shooting the pictures was a rather cumbersome process. We'd taken the stop off the side window so we could open it to prevent glare on the film, and Nevin had rigged up a clamp to go on the door after the window was opened. Mind you, we were doing over 100 miles per hour! Sometimes Nevin even put the camera and part of his head out the window into the wind stream, and I noticed how his muscles bulged as he strained to hold on to the device. Originally, we'd planned to rotate our roles of flying and picture-taking, but I decided I'd better have a talk with Nevin about it, knowing my body wouldn't be happy taking pictures. That night in our hotel in New Orleans, I told him there was a change in plans. "I'll fly the airplane. You take the pictures. However many days it takes, I'll refund them to you by letting you fly twice to my one."

The second day we covered a distance of 623 miles, landing for the night in Pecos, Texas, where we were interviewed by a news reporter. That was another of Nevin's excellent contributions, contacting news organizations in advance to ensure media attention and publicity for Angel Flight.

On our way to Arizona, day three's destination, we flew over impressive Texas landscapes, including Guadalupe Peak, the highest natural point in the state. I'd planned to make a landing in Tombstone, Arizona, where Barbara and I had been a couple of years before and enjoyed a tourist favorite, the reenactment of the gunfight at the OK Corral. Unfortunately, a gigantic thunderstorm was sitting right over Tombstone, so Nevin and I went to Tucson instead and took aerial pictures of the largest stockpile of retired aircraft in the world, the Davis Monthan Boneyard. We also photographed the studios where movies of the Old West were, and still are, filmed. We landed, then went to our hotel and headed downstairs for dinner. Suddenly, a booming thunderclap stopped us in our tracks, followed by torrents of rain. The ferocious storm put out the lights throughout the city for about five hours. This meant, of course, that dinner couldn't be cooked, so the restaurant staff brought out perishables and everyone got to eat for free. After leaving Arizona, we went to Southern California, landing at John Wayne Airport, and spent the night in a nearby motel. My cousin Donna Bennett Cole from Orange came over and joined us for dinner.

The biggest thrill of our journey came the next morning, on day four, when we landed in Victorville, California, in the Mojave Desert. When I touched down at SCLA (Southern California Logistics Airport), I was overcome with nostalgia. I could make out the patterns and the outline of the old, original runway, the one I would land the B-24s on when it was an army airfield. "The last time I put a rubber mark on this runway was seventy years ago," I said on the tower frequency, tears welling in my eyes.

Somebody in another airplane on the frequency responded in disbelief, saying, "Did you say 'seven zero' years back?" In my mind, the more than 100 commercial and corporate jets parked for service and repair became the B-24 bombers that were there for the same purpose, only then, when I was head of one of the maintenance squadrons, it was for battle-readiness.

When we arrived at the FBO and Million Air, the CEO came out and greeted us. We were also met by a film crew and reporters from two radio stations. They took us around to show us the original area, now in a state of collapse. I explained the history of various old, dilapidated buildings from my era and told them that some days were so hot in Victorville, we'd leave footprints in the blacktop. The original hangars were still there and in pretty good shape. Leaving Victorville that day for Santa Ana, where we planned to spend the night, I chewed on the idea that our own personal histories are entangled in the present, and though buildings fall down and our tracks are erased in the sand, we carry within us the reality of all we've ever experienced and what can never be taken away. On day five we flew across the Mojave Desert, avoiding restrictive air spaces, and eventually reached the coast, then landed at the Santa Ana Airport. There, I enjoyed a lengthy visit with my nephew, Roger Appel, and the refreshment of breezes coming off the Pacific Ocean.

The rest of the trip took us to the Pacific Coast for some shoreline shots and then inland where we'd hoped to photograph the San Francisco Harbor, Golden Gate Bridge, and Alcatraz, but dense fog made the conditions too risky to get down closer. We flew inland and made our way to Oregon where my brother-in-law had a summer home and hosted us for three rewarding nights. After such a pleasant rest, we were ready for more adventure. This time we soared above mountains: Mount Hood in Oregon, and in Washington, Mount St. Helen's, Mount Adams, and Mount Rainer. The views were spectacular. The next day, day eight of flight, "we said goodbye to the Rocky Mountain Range and hello to the Big Sky of Montana," as Nevin expressed it so colorfully on the Wings Around America website. Day nine was in Sioux Falls, South Dakota, where we saw the Crazy Horse, Mt. Rushmore, and Little Big Horn monuments.

We spent two nights in Sioux Falls to recoup. It so happened my ninety-second birthday fell on August 7, and I was treated to a grand celebration at Landmark Aviation. From there we flew to Green Bay Packers' territory in Wisconsin and another green landmark, the fifty-foot statue of the Jolly Green Giant. He happened to be wearing his Relay for Life T-shirt when we took his picture from the air. We traveled to Michigan and admired the beautiful Mackinac suspension bridge, known as the "Mighty Mac," that connects the upper and lower peninsulas. Another rush of nostalgia came when we flew over Willow Run east of Ypsilanti where more than 8,600 B-24 Liberator bombers had been manufactured, with one produced every hour. To think that I most likely flew some of the B-24s made in that factory!

And then it was Day 12, with only one more day until we arrived back home in Virginia. We followed the Lake Erie coastline, flying over the magnificent Sandusky Bay Bridge in Ohio and over Cleveland, then on to Erie, Pennsylvania, and New York State, where we were given permission to fly to the falls on the Canadian side, perfect for Nevin and his Nikon Coolpix P510. He was able to get quite close for some fantastic photographs.

On our last day, August 10, we took off from Niagara International Airport and returned to the falls on the American side for pictures, then headed home. We'd planned on arriving in Luray at a specific time, and when we were about half an hour out, I realized we'd get there too soon, that people would be waiting to welcome us, so I pulled the power back and ran slow for a while, arriving at 2:00 p.m., as agreed. What a homecoming it was! We were greeted with a big sign that read, "Welcome Home, Cross Country Angels!" and received hugs and smiles from family and friends.

All totaled, we flew a distance of 5,758 nautical miles for 56.6 hours. For all thirteen days of flight, we were VFR because we didn't want to be on a fixed altitude. It was the trip of a lifetime, giving us opportunity to raise money and influence for Angel Flight, to see both the rugged and tamed contours of this great country, and to meet new friends everywhere we went. It allowed me to travel back in time to a period of my life when America needed me and men like me and trained us for lethal warfare from the sky. It was the best, most comprehensive training any aviator could ever have, and my crew in the B-24 for bombing and OSS missions were the best men. Only I survive, but I carry them on the wings of my heart.

Epilogue

It's a mystery to me how the past can show up unexpectedly and like something shiny new, with its rag-tag band of memories following behind. That's what happened to me. I had the good fortune to be reunited with many of the men who had flown with me in the B-24. The most significant of these reunions was with the man who would become my best friend, Fred Mayer. This meeting wouldn't have taken place if not for a reunion that preceded it. After the war, Dick Gottleber, the bombardier, and I kept up with each other, exchanging letters and the occasional long-distance phone call. I suggested we meet in person, and he happily agreed to host me and my family. So I loaded up the '65 Plymouth with Nancy, Leslie, Lee, and luggage, and we drove all the way from Mt. Vernon, Virginia, to Saginaw, Michigan. His wife, Lenore, answered the door, with Dick right behind looking just the same, only a pound or two heavier and a little grayer.

As we were sitting around the table after dinner, Dick says, "Have you spoken to Fred yet?"

"Fred?" I said. "Fred who?"

"Fred Mayer, of course."

"Who's he?"

As you will recall, when I flew OSS missions the identity of agents was kept secret. They were all "Joes" to me. The only information I had after the Operation Greenup drop was that the mission was successful. Everything else about it was classified for ten years after the war. So, when Dick told me who Fred was and that he lived in Charles Town, West Virginia, I was astounded. Dick gave me his address. It had so happened that during one of the down days in Italy during the war while waiting for the go-ahead on Operation Greenup, Dick "practiced" his German on Fred, but the real purpose was to exchange their hometown addresses. These they committed to their excellent memories instead of writing them down.

EPILOGUE

After the war, Fred went back to his civilian job as a diesel engineer. He worked all over the world for the Voice of America until his retirement twenty years later. That's when he went to Michigan to find Dick. They stayed in touch, and now I would have the joy of finding Fred. On my way home from Michigan, I went by Charles Town (West Virginia is about an hour and a half from Mt. Vernon) and located his house. Eagerly, I rang the doorbell. No answer. I rang again but no one answered, so I left a note with my name and phone number. The next morning – a Wednesday – the phone rang and a voice said, "Hello, John!" And then Fred told me that I would be coming to his house for lunch.

That Friday, Nancy and I drove to Fred's house. It's hard to put into words what I felt when I saw him. It was an instant and extraordinary bond, a closer-than-a-brother feeling. During our visit, he took off his shirt to show me his back. It looked like a map of railroad tracks. When I expressed my dismay over his scars, he said his back didn't bother him anymore because "I don't have to look at it."

The story of his torture at the hands of the Gestapo is painful to hear, but it reveals the character of the man without a fear nerve. After his many successes as an OSS agent foiling Nazi operations, he was betrayed by a liaison who worked the black market. At the time Fred was posing as a French laborer and operating from the home of Franz Weber's sister. Then came the scary knock that changed everything. In his book *This Grim and Savage Game,* Tom Snow gives a graphic account of Fred's treatment at the hands of the Nazis who burst into the house, armed with submachine guns:

> *In the dark room, the Gestapo officers slapped and punched the spy in the face. His cover wasn't holding water, and so the tall one stripped him from head to toe. Despite the agent's bullish strength, the SS men brutally manhandled him, shoving him to the floor. Cuffing his hands in front of him and pulling his arms over his bent knees, they forced him into a constricting fetal position, then shoved the barrel of a long rifle into the tiny gap behind his knees and his cuffed hands. With a man on each side of the rifle, they lifted his naked, rolled-up body and suspended the human ball between two tables, like a piece of meat on a skewer. Uncoiling a rawhide whip, the tall one put his full weight behind each swing, mercilessly thrashing the agent's body like a side of beef.*

Fred told me that Gunter, the interrogator – "a little rat" he called him – jammed a Luger into his mouth, then hit him with a haymaker, breaking all four back molars. He never broke. Not only that, he actually brought about the Nazi surrender of Innsbruck, pretending to have authority to arrest his captor, Franz Hofer, the governor of Tyrol in what was called one of the great bluffs of the war. There's no telling how many lives were saved because of Fred's fearless actions and intelligence. William Casey, the former CIA head, called Operation Greenup "by far the most successful of OSS operations" in southern Europe. The entire real-life drama is documented in a film I was proud to be part of, *The Real Inglorious Bastards,* mentioned in Chapter Eight.

The next time I saw Fred was at a reunion of our OSS crew. Here's how it came about. Lenore Gottleber was a woman on a mission. She and Dick had married after the war and lived in Saginaw. Lenore launched on a campaign to find out who from the OSS crew was still living and where they lived. (With OSS missions, there was naturally no need for a bombardier, so Dick rode in the front turret and became the pilotage navigator.) Once Lenore had gathered the desired information, she and Dick organized a reunion, what Jim O'Flarity called "The First Annual B-24 Reunion."

Actually, I'd run into Jim before the reunion in a most surprising way. I was flying for Eastern en route to New York and, as was my custom, had greeted the passengers over the intercom, introducing myself as Captain Billings. During the trip, the flight attendant came to the cockpit and said, "Do you know James O'Flarity?" She looked about fifteen, and I'm thinking, "How does she know that name?"

"Why?" I asked her.

"Some guy back there says he flew with you during the war."

"Go back there and tell him to get his ass up here!"

And then he was there, my tail gunner in the B-24, ole Jim O'Flarity himself! "Sit down here," I told him. Back in those days we could invite visitors to the cockpit. Jim and I talked up a storm until we landed. Once on the ground, I jumped out to say goodbye to the passengers as I always did. Jim introduced me to his wife, Betty, and we exchanged contact information and promised to get together.

During that same month, I had a trip to Boston and went into the airport to do the necessary paperwork for outbound. Afterward, I walked upstairs to get a snack in the gate area and who do you suppose was there but Jim O'Flarity! "We're gonna have a reunion," I told him and explained how Dick and Lenore wanted to get the crew together in their home.

EPILOGUE

Well, they had the reunion, and it was an intensely emotional experience. Everyone was there except for two crew members. One was Daniel Halperin, my rear side gunner. He never returned from Europe as far as any of us knew. The other missing person was my co-pilot, Roland Nix, who Lenore learned had died. This of course filled me with great sadness. Naturally we were all older and heavier, but we were the same band of brothers. We eagerly brought out our photos from the war and relived our adventures through stories, gestures, and expressions that needed no words.

We met again the next year at Fred's invitation in Harper's Ferry, West Virginia, where we were treated to rooms at Cliffside Motel to celebrate his eightieth birthday. For this reunion, the other Greenup team members were present. Franz Weber and Hans Wynbert flew from Europe to Washington, D.C., and rented a car to Harper's Ferry. The OSS radio dispatcher Walter Hass came from Florida. A newspaper reporter showed up to cover our historic gathering. But to prove we weren't stuck in the past, we went to the Charles Town race track and bet on the horses. What did it matter that nobody won?

Other reunions have followed through the years, including those of the 484th and 461st Bombardment Groups. The first of these was held in Colorado Springs, sometime in the late Sixties. I remember my amazement when the phone rang and it was Glen Sandberg, the ball turret gunner who'd been so afraid of getting smashed to pieces if the plane was struck and the turret didn't retract. "I heard about the reunion and I'm going," he said. The entire 44th bomb group was there, with over 500 people attending, including wives and children. Glen and I spent practically every minute together. Sadly, before the next reunion he died.

In the early years, some of these reunions drew nearly 700 people. There would always be a memorabilia room, and among the curios you'd sometimes see parts from B-24s. As time went on, the numbers in attendance dwindled, and other bomb groups were added to fill the hotels. The last reunion I attended was in Dallas in 2019, and all the bomb groups from the 15th Air Force were there, with a total of 300 people in attendance. Of these, only twenty-five of us were Second World War veterans. The rest were family and friends. Because of Covid-19, the 2020 reunion was cancelled. I've been hearing that the next reunion, tentatively scheduled for 2021 in Albuquerque, will include anybody from the 15th Air Force, not just members of a bomb group. It makes you wonder who will be left. It's always hard leaving these reunions as you're very aware that it might be the last time you see some of your brothers.

Appendix A

Career Summary

Active Duty: Dec. 1942 – June 1947

Combat in B-24s based in Italy: August 1944 – May 1945

14 bombing missions: 484th Bomb Group (825th Bomb Squadron)

39 OSS missions: 885th Heavy Special Squadron

Post-Combat

B-24 engineering test at Victorville Army Air Field (Mojave Desert, California)

General Aviation

June 1946 to present

Flight and Ground Instructor

August 1946 – June 1948

Airline Aviation

TWA: June 1947 – June 1948 (DC-3)

Eastern Airlines: July 1948 – August 1983

Douglas DC-3, DC-4, DC-6, DC-7, DC-9

Martin 404, Convair 440

Lockheed Constellation and Electra

Angel Flight: 2005 – present (459 missions)

Missions: 459 and counting

Total flying hours: 29,600

Appendix B

Medals, Citations, and Awards

1945

Distinguished Flying Cross

Air Medal with four oak leaf clusters

Presidential Unit Citation (885th Heavy Special Bombardment Squadron)

Special Recognition Citation (Retired Eastern Airlines Pilot Association)

Hall of Fame (Retired Eastern Airlines Pilot Association)

Federal Aviation Administration (Wright Brothers Master Pilot Award)

2009

Angel Flight Mid-Atlantic (AFMA): Virginia Pilot of the Year

2011

AFMA Virginia Pilot of the Year

2013

AFMA Pilot of the Year (Mid-Atlantic Region)

Smithsonian Walk of Fame

2014

AFMA Pilot of the Year (Mid-Atlantic Region)

2015

Endeavor Award (Angel Flight West)

SPECIAL DUTIES PILOT

2016

AFMA Lifetime Achievement Award

Special Services Association Lifetime Honorary Membership

The OSS Society Distinguished Service Award

2017

National Aeronautical Association Distinguished Volunteer Pilot

2018

OSS Congressional Gold Medal

AFMA Virginia Pilot of the Year

AFMA Pilot of the Year (Mid-Atlantic Region)

Citation from Frank Borman, Apollo 8

Presidential Unit Citation Medal

Daughters of the American Revolution (DAR) Medal of Honor

Appendix C

Member Organizations

484th Wing Bomb Group Association (Board of Directors)

801st/492nd Bombardment Group Association ("Carpetbaggers")

Aircraft Owners and Pilots Association

Air Force Association

Air Line Pilots Association (Treasurer)

American Legion

Experimental Aircraft Association

Mensa

National Rifle Association

National Skeet Shooting Association (Treasurer)

Retired Eastern Pilots Association (Treasurer)

The OSS Society

United Flying Octogenarians

Veterans of Foreign Wars

Index